Staying Together

When an Affair Pulls You Apart

Stephen M. Judah, Ph.D.

IVP Books

An imprint of InterVarsity Press
Downers Grove, Illinois

InterVarsity Press
P.O. Box 1400, Downers Grove, IL 60515-1426
World Wide Web: www.ivpress.com
E-mail: mail@ivpress.com

©2006 by Stephen M. Judah

InterVarsity Press® is the book-publishing division of InterVarsity Christian Fellowship/USA®, a student movement active on campus at hundreds of universities, colleges and schools of nursing in the United States of America, and a member movement of the International Fellowship of Evangelical Students. For information about local and regional activities, write Public Relations Dept., InterVarsity Christian Fellowship/USA, 6400 Schroeder Rd., P.O. Box 7895, Madison, WI 53707-7895, or visit the IVCF website at <www.intervarsity.org>.

All Scripture quotations, unless otherwise indicated, are taken from the Holy Bible, New International Version®. NIV®. Copyright ©1973, 1978, 1984 by International Bible Society. Used by permission of Zondervan Publishing House. All rights reserved.

Design: Cindy Kiple
Images: knotted rope: Steve Bronstein / Getty Images
       rope pulling apart: Christine Balderas / istock photo

ISBN-10: 0-8308-3399-4
ISBN-13: 978-0-8308-3399-3

Printed in the United States of America ∞

Library of Congress Cataloging-in-Publication Data

Judah, Stephen M., 1949-
  Staying together when an affair pulls you apart / Stephen M. Judah.
     p. cm.
  Includes bibliographical references.
  ISBN-13: 978-0-8308-3399-3 (pbk.: alk. paper)
  ISBN-10: 0-8308-3399-4 (pbk.: alk. paper)
  1. Marriage—Religious aspects—Christianity. 2. Adultery. I.
Title.
BV835.J83 2006
248.8'44—dc22

                                             2006013025

P   19 18 17 16 15 14 13 12 11 10 9 8 7 6 5 4 3 2 1

Y   21 20 19 18 17 16 15 14 13 12 11 10 09 08 07 06

To my parents, wife, children and friends
who always believed in me.

To my clients
who in believing overcame infidelity.

Contents

Introduction

A couple bond and marry. Then they encounter negative traits in each other that do not easily change, and their bond begins to break. One of them has an affair, which provides evidence of that break and furthers the brokenness between them.

If you ask people having an affair if they like who they've become they might answer, "I've done something and become someone I'd never imagine." Affairs are not simply a breach in a relationship; they also reflect brokenness within the individual.

The Bible uses the metaphor of infidelity to describe the broken relationship between humans and God. Perhaps affairs at their core are about the brokenness between God and us.

God gave Moses the Ten Commandments, enduring and globally accepted principles to live by, and included among them the commandment to not commit adultery. This commandment speaks to the relationship between a man and a woman, but alongside this commandment is God's command to have no other god before him. Infidelity goes beyond the act of adultery alone. When people value anything (children, money, success, drugs, even themselves) more than God, they become an infidel—which is to say, they become broken.

People who don't believe in God aren't off the hook; substitute the concept of conscience, wisdom, altruism or love for God, and infidelity still functions as a breach. At some time in some way all of us have become infidels. Infidelity is about brokenness. This is—and is not —a spiritual book.

You may have started to read this book because you find yourself in an affair. By contrast you may suspect or know that your partner is having an affair. Most books I've read about infidelity either provide an autobiographical journey through someone's struggle or offer clinical perspectives on the phenomenon. In most such books I've found some good suggestions, but often they lacked what I'd call a strategic synthesis.

Staying Together When an Affair Pulls You Apart will provide that strategic synthesis. It will be useful to the everyday couple and the professional who counsels them. After orienting you to the terrain, we will examine the primary causes of infidelity. Next I will examine the stages of infidelity stretching from childhood into adulthood. Finally, we will examine key steps to safely and rapidly overcome infidelity. Imbedded in those key steps are five essential disciplines for moving relationships toward wholeness.

CLEARING THE PATH

Once I was hiking on a mountain trail when a powerful wind swept through. I was both afraid of and mesmerized by the force of wind. I was glad to be above the treeline, where I wouldn't have to be worried about being hit by dead limbs and branches blown out of the trees.

The force of the wind actually serves a vital purpose for the trees: it removes broken and decayed branches, permitting the new and strong—the whole—to grow.

When you finish this book, you will not only possess the tools for overcoming infidelity, you will have begun mastering the tools for creating whole relationships—with your partner, your family members, your coworkers, even yourself. Perhaps along the way you will also encounter God as a transforming force—removing your brokenness and empowering you toward wholeness.

When you're caught up in the turmoil of an affair, however, it's hard to see the forest for the trees. Recovery requires a broad or panoramic view. I'd like to view it as a journey up and down a mountain. We ascend into brokenness; we descend into wholeness.

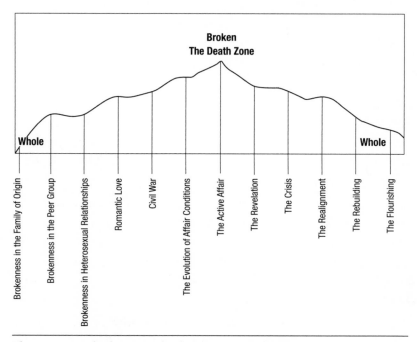

The ascent into brokenness, the descent into wholeness.

THE ASCENT INTO BROKENNESS

The roots of infidelity actually reach into childhood. People finish childhood with personality traits or unmet needs that factor into the likelihood of infidelity. As a simple example, a child who is ignored in some way may experience an intensified yearning for connection or recognition. Often this feature endures for a long time, and if that yearning is not fulfilled in primary relationships, the person will seek it out in secondary relationships.

Similarly, the patterns of early childhood development may repeat in peer or same-sex relationships. The child who dominated his or her siblings or parents may tend to dominate playmates and class-mates. If the child was dominated the reverse holds true, with impli-cations for adult relationships.

Dating relationships provide yet another opportunity for the pat-tern to repeat. By this time the need for approval, or the sense of con-fidence, or whatever the enduring trait, appears universally ingrained and plays out in early dating relationships.

Dating relationships often lead to couples getting married or living together. A sense of romance permeates these experiences. Partners tend to be similar on the surface (race, for example, or age or level of education) but often you discover that underneath the surface your spouse is more similar to your parents.

Enduring differences—traits and patterns that seem offensive, painful and irreconcilable—lead to a kind of civil war in the relation-ship. Brokenness persists until it is recognized and resolved. Unre-solved, however, the developmental flaws between the couple cause their bond to weaken. Struggles with communication, conflict reso-lution and the pressures of the moment further hasten the disintegra-tion of the bond. Pressures build up in the relationship, and finally reach an explosive intensity.

Since we are both social and sexual in nature, this pressurization frequently follows a social and sexual path—an affair. At the peak of adulthood you may find yourself and your partner in a broken mess. You have climbed into a fragile, yet rugged, and threatening environ-ment. You have ascended into brokenness.

THE DESCENT INTO WHOLENESS

Regaining true and complete wholeness requires the revelation of the affair. Sometimes the affair reveals itself; other times the offending spouse confesses the affair. The intensity of the pressures involved, the sudden shift in the world as you know it, causes disorganization and confusion—a crisis. That crisis provides the opportunity to descend back into wholeness.

There are lots of decisions to be made at this point. Offending spouses must choose to align with either their marital partner or the third party. Offended spouses must choose to align with or break from the offending spouse. The third party must choose to hold onto or let go of the offending spouse. And the biggest decision involves how each person reconciles their decisions with their personal core values.

Most people who seek and receive good counsel choose to rebuild their marriage. Those who do so using sound plans and tools end up with a superior structure, a better relationship, compared to that which existed before. The process of rebuilding takes time, involves both cost and effort, but the reward speaks volumes. If the married couple has not substantially transformed their relationship, they will likely be doomed to repeat their history.

Too many relationships use all their resources simply struggling to survive. The descent into wholeness goes to a different place. It is a place where people and relationships thrive and flourish. It is a place where people and relationships have resources to share. It is a place of security and significance. I invite you to follow a path with me through this book toward wholeness.

PART ONE

Know the Terrain

Contours of Affairs

Attitudes, Frequency and Social Impact

Long before climbing a mountain, wise climbers familiarize themselves with it. They look at photos or view it in person. They know the length of the approach trail, the length of the ascent path, the gain in vertical elevation, the interaction with the weather and seasons, and all the unique dangers associated with the mountain. They get to know the contours of the mountain as protection against a climbing tragedy. Similarly, knowing the features and contours of infidelity in and of itself may save some couples from a marital tragedy.

A 2001 Gallup poll found that 91 percent of Americans consider it to be either always or almost always wrong for married people to have sexual relations with someone other than their spouses. In response to a separate but related question, 89 percent say that "married men and women having an affair" is morally unacceptable.[1]

Western marriage vows include some variation of the phrase "I take you to have and to hold from this day forth, for better for worse, for richer for poorer, in sickness and in health, to love and to cherish till death us do part, and thereto I pledge you my faith." In the formal ceremony of marriage we publicly declare our faithfulness—our fidelity. We mean it when we say it, don't we? What goes wrong?

THE PERVASIVENESS OF INFIDELITY

How many people violate their expressed vow of fidelity? Lots, although no one can get a firm handle on how many people stray. The estimates vary widely. Two prolific researchers on sexuality and infidelity, David Buss and Todd Shackelford, summarized nine relevant empirical studies on the frequency of infidelity:[2]

- Affairs over the course of marriage range from 30 to 60 percent for men, from 20 to 50 percent for women.
- The combined probability that at least one member of a married couple will have an affair over the course of a marriage ranges from 40 to 76 percent.

A conservative interpretation of these figures suggests perhaps half of all married couples will experience infidelity over the course of their marriage. Cohabitation research consistently reveals even higher rates for infidelity.

The likelihood of infidelity tends to increase over time. A nationwide study of 3,432 asked the question "Have you ever had sex with someone other than your husband or wife while you were married?"[3]

- 7.1 percent of men ages 18-29 answered yes
- 20.5 percent of men ages 30-39 answered yes
- 31.4 percent of men ages 40-49 answered yes
- 37 percent of men ages 50-59 answered yes
- 11.7 percent of women ages 18-29 answered yes
- 14.5 percent of women ages 30-39 answered yes
- 19.9 percent of women ages 40-49 answered yes
- 12 percent of women ages 50-59 answered yes

Put more simply:

- By the tenth anniversary, approximately 10 percent of men and 10 percent of women have had an affair.
- By the twentieth anniversary, approximately 20 percent of men and 15 percent of women have had an affair.

- By the thirtieth anniversary, approximately 30 percent of men and 20 percent of women have had an affair.
- By the fortieth anniversary, approximately 40 percent of men and 25 percent of women have had an affair.

Pioneering infidelity researcher Shirley Glass reviewed 25 studies and concluded that 25 percent of wives and 44 percent of husbands have had extramarital intercourse in the course of their life. She further adds that the inclusion of emotional affairs would increase these totals by 15-20 percent.[4]

Research still has a long way to go in this arena.[5] The definition of infidelity poses challenges. Consider the variation between a sexual affair, an emotional affair and erotic contact not involving intercourse.

THE GEOGRAPHY OF INFIDELITY

Eight percent of married adults from major cities in the United States report having extramarital sex within the previous year. Contrast that with 2 percent from rural areas and 4 percent from the suburbs.[6] Given these statistics possibly one out of every 12.5 married adults living in large cities engage in an extramarital affair in the course of a year. At first this statistic may seem mysterious. My guess is that the simple rule of proximity largely explains this.

I grew up in a rural area of southwestern Indiana. As a senior in high school I took a solo train trip to Washington, D.C., by way of Chicago. As I walked around Chicago I encountered strip clubs for the first time. Later I did postgraduate training in Manhattan. In my hotel room I encountered adult shows on TV for the first time. Perhaps there were adult films and strip clubs in southwestern Indiana, but in a rural setting they're out of view; in a big city they're in plain sight.

Then there is the other world to consider—the cyber world. Cyber affairs may not involve direct touch at all. Nevertheless, the data are shocking.

- 57 percent of people have used the Internet to flirt
- 38 percent of people have engaged in explicit online sexual conversation
- 50 percent of people have made phone contact with someone they chatted with online
- 31 percent of people have had an online conversation that has led to real-time sex[7]

When I first started counseling, no Internet existed. Now it is rare for it not to play a role in the complex of infidelity. The Internet lets us interact like nothing else. We can interact with one person or multitudes in the room next to us or around the world. We have closeted access to every disturbing perversion imaginable. I can be minding my own business when an e-mail abruptly invites me to enhance my sexual performance or contact some eager-to-please partner. Evidence supports the prevalence of disinhibition, accelerated intimacy and hypersexual behavior in online settings. There is a high correlation between online cybersex and subsequent real-time sexual affairs.[8] Clearly all this plays a role in increasing the risk of infidelity.

HEALTH IMPACT

An OB-GYN in suburban Columbus, Ohio, reports that 1 to 2 percent of his practice population have a life-threatening STD; 25 percent have a less serious STD. Another OB-GYN in northeast Columbus reports treating on average eight cases per day of unexplained STD. The conversation goes like this:

"Based on our lab results I need to report that you tested positive for a sexually transmitted disease. Is this explainable given your pattern of sexual activity?"

The patient answers yes or no. If no the next question comes: "Is this explainable given what you know about the sexual activity of your partner?"

Again the patient answers yes or no. "As your physician I need to advise you to discuss this with your partner. If your partner remains an infected carrier we may be wasting our time treating only you."

Sexually transmitted diseases present a range of health challenges and might be considered a pandemic.

- Acquired Immune Deficiency Syndrome (AIDS) has caused 886,575 total cases and 501,669 deaths in the United States from 1981 to 2002.[9] Approximately 40,000 new HIV infections occur each year in the United States, 70 percent of them among men and 30 percent among women.

- Herpes Simplex Virus (HSV) causes a million new cases of herpes per year in the United States.[10] According to the U.S. Centers for Disease Control and Prevention, 45 million people in the United States ages 12 and older, or 1 out of 5 of the total adolescent and adult population, are infected with HSV-2. Nationwide, since the late 1970s, the number of people with genital herpes infection has increased 30 percent.

- Chlamydia is diagnosed in three million new cases per year in the United States.[11] You can get genital chlamydial infection during oral, vaginal or anal sexual contact with an infected partner. It can cause serious problems in men and women, as well as in newborn babies of infected mothers. Left untreated it can cause two serious illnesses: pelvic inflammatory disease (PID) in women and epidydimitis (inflammation of the reproductive area near the testicles) in men.

- Human Papaloma Virus (HPV) is diagnosed in five million new cases per year in the United States.[12] HPV predisposes women to cervical cancer, is difficult to detect and is currently incurable. Current research shows that condom use does not prevent the transmission of HPV during sexual activity.

Safe sex as a public health policy has a valuable purpose. However, based on the data it's safe to say that safe sex is an oxymoron.[13]

SUMMARY

Infidelity, as we have seen, has a significant footprint. Researchers have found that infidelity was a primary or contributing factor in approximately one-third of divorce cases.[14] In an ethnographic study of 160 cultures, Laura Betzig reported that out of a list of forty-three causes of divorce, infidelity was the single most frequently cited cause.[15] Divorce after indfidelity is more likely when (1) the infidelity is known to the betrayed partner, (2) the wife is the unfaithful spouse, (3) the occurrence takes place early in the marriage, and (4) the extramarital involvement was both sexual and emotional in nature.[16]

More important is the crisis that infidelity creates in your personal world. Hopefully this brief examination of broad demographic features has introduced you to the contours of infidelity. Now we'll examine particular types of affairs in more depth.

— 2 —

Types of Affairs

Both mountains and affairs form as a result of enormous pressures. Five types of mountains have been identified: dome, fold, fault-block, volcanic and plateau. You can almost picture the mountain in the name of the type. Similarly three types of extramarital affairs have been identified. The name of each type says something about how they formed or about their extent. The professional jargon refers to affairs as

- sexual (involving intercourse)
- nonpenetrating (involving sexual or erotic contact, such as kissing or fondling, but not actual intercourse)
- mental (the affair of the heart)

The first two types are pretty straightforward; a mental affair occurs when a new partner replaces your spouse as the primary partner in your mind. This can occur through private thoughts alone, or may include verbal or written interaction.

Infidelity involves sequential escalation.

Anyone who looks at a woman lustfully has already committed adultery with her in his heart. (Matthew 5:28)

Each one is tempted when, by his own evil desire, he is dragged away and enticed. Then, after desire has conceived, it gives birth to sin; and sin, when it is full-grown, gives birth to death. (James 1:14-15)

Do you see the sequence in these verses? Applied to the extramarital affair, they might be understood as follows:

1. Looking at another person with desire may lead to an affair of the heart.

2. Affairs of the heart may lead to some type of physical relationship—a nonpenetrating affair.

3. A nonpenetrating affair often leads to intercourse—a sexual affair.

The sequence of escalation repeats itself in almost every movie script. The pair exchange glances, their eyes meet, and they briefly smile. They talk casually and begin an acquaintance. Over time their conversations become ever so gently yet progressively more personal, then clearly intimate. The kiss and embrace. They taste connection. Soon enough in more private environments they touch more intimately and perhaps sexually. Eventually, in some way death— the death of a marriage, the death of innocence, the death of conscience—starts creeping in.

All types of infidelity complicate, disrupt or even break your connection and bond with your spouse. In some cases, however, the bond between the husband and the wife has already been broken— the affair only confirms and exacerbates it. Lust and desire conceive and ultimately give birth to death.

I define *infidelity* as a relationship with anyone other than your spouse which is sexual or intensely relational in nature, and secret. So one finds three components:

- extramarital
- sexual or intensely relational
- secret

DIFFERENT VARIATIONS, SIMILAR IMPACT

There are a variety of scenarios in the different types of affairs. Offenders often justify their particular infidelity by concentrating on what it was not.

Secret fantasy. Sophia and her husband came to me for counseling. Sophia reported weekly going to her basement and masturbating to her favorite TV show (*MacGyver*). The impact on the marriage relationship amounted to the functional equivalent of sexually acting out with an actual person.

A secret fantasy of an affair may carry the emotional weight of an actual affair.[1] Though it primarily involved fantasy, Sophia's husband still struggled with jealousy and Sophia grieved the loss of her secret, fantasy lover as they began to work toward eventual reconciliation.

We just talked. Tammy wanted to train for a marathon. Her neighbor, who had run several, agreed to run with her to establish a training routine. They ran and talked multiple days each week over several months. Now the neighbor has initiated his divorce, and Tammy has informed her husband, Troy, "I'm only open to a platonic relationship with you at this time." Tammy has not yet decided to divorce but vows never to be sexually active again with Troy.

We touched, but we never had sex. Emily and Dean have been married fifteen years and have three young children. They've had some conflicts, but just over a year ago Emily remained eager to restore their marriage. With Dean only half-heartedly focused on restoration and brushing off Emily's attempts with the phrase "I guess I'm just boring," Emily began to talk to a male friend at church. He listened to her and valued her for who she was. They prayed together. In time they kissed and embraced. They bonded. Now she's determined to leave her marriage.

It was just straight sex. Phil said "I've never had an affair. I've gone to gentlemen's clubs and have had sex a few times with the ladies there. But I've never gotten involved emotionally." To Phil, emotional involvement defined an affair.

Wherever a couple falls in the sequence of infidelity—mental, nonpenetrating, sexual—the infidelity alters the relationship. Few life experiences affect a relationship more forcefully.

GENDER DIFFERENCES

Men and women approach infidelity differently. Men seem to get drawn predominately to the sexual part of infidelity, women to the relational part. Sociolinguist Deborah Tannen observes that

> women speak and hear a language of connection and intimacy, while men speak and hear a language of status and independence. . . . Boys tend to play outside in large groups that are hierarchically structured. . . . Boys' games have winners and losers. . . . Girls . . . play in small groups or in pairs; the center of a girl's social life is a best friend.[2]

Some women seek relationship with other women and bond so tightly that their relationship functions as infidelity. They may or may not act out sexually, but the marriage gets disrupted. In the face of their husband's sexual affair, I often hear women say, "The sex part doesn't bother me so much. What really hurts is that our marital bond has been broken." Men, on the other hand, get more hurt or incensed about the sexual infidelity of their spouse. I once had to tackle a man who lunged to attack his wife upon hearing of her sexual infidelity. In a transient homicidal rage he had to be hospitalized.

These sex differences can be combined to better understand and define the level of risk caused by the infidelity:

Lower-risk infidelity (stage I): Infidelity involving only sex *or* relationship—not both.

Higher-risk infidelity (stage II): Infidelity involving *both* sex and relationship.

A woman who acts out sexually may be experiencing both a relational bond plus a sexual bond, whereas a man who acts out sexually may be experiencing only a sexual bond. Consequently, even though both affairs are sexual, one may be at higher risk for divorce. Of course, lower-risk infidelity over time with the same person may progress to stage II.

Jordan worked as a commercial paint contractor. He told me he typically preferred having sex with prostitutes who would do anything sexually to get money for their next drug fix. His marriage, though not fulfilling, would not be terminated by him. He was at stage I. Then he met an extramarital partner whom he enjoyed relationally. He progressed to stage II and moved out of his home. His twenty-year marriage was now at risk of termination.

The classification system in table 2.1 identifies the risk and complexity of infidelity by combining the key dimensions of both sex and relationship. The left side identifies the level or nature of the relationship. The right side identifies the level of sexual involvement. The two numbers are added together to determine the degree of severity and complexity for any given situation. For example, exchanging sexual words (3) with an employee or coworker (4) reaches a combined rank of 7; intercourse (6) with a prostitute (1) also ranks at 7.[3]

Table 2.1. Relationship and Sexual Continuum

Relationship Level	Rank	Sexual Level
6. Family Member	**12.** Highest	6. Intercourse
5. Friend	**10.** High	5. Erotic Contact
4. Employee / Coworker	**8.** Medium	4. Frequent/prolonged nonerotic touch
3. Neighbor	**6.** Medium	3. Sexual Words
2. Acquaintance	**4.** Low	2. Pictures and Photos
1. Prostitute or Pick Up	**2.** Lowest	1. Fantasy

The biblical King David was initially at low risk of an affair with Bathsheba; they were at best neighbors, and David was unilaterally indulging a fantasy, scoring a 4. But they quickly escalated to a 10 when he brought her to his home for intercourse (2 Samuel 11). In contrast, the biblical patriarch Joseph was at high risk of infidelity with his employer's wife (9), which explains his employer's extreme response but makes his own restraint all the more remarkable (Genesis 39).

VARIATIONS FROM THE COMMON GENDER DIFFERENCES

The sex or gender differences between men and women create patterns, tendencies and probabilities, but variations certainly occur. And some of the variations have their own story to tell.

Celeste and her husband had a volatile relationship. In a private session she revealed to me that she was molested beginning at age twelve by her uncle and a twenty-year-old cousin. She has had about fifty sex partners, and she stole about $30,000 from her last employer, a jeweler. She mostly purchased clothes and accessories with the money. Her husband had no idea of this.

Sexually promiscuous women often have a history of some form of sexual abuse. The early sexual abuse in some cases seems to rewire the identity of these women and link it to hypersexuality. Some promiscuous women, however, have a history of a far more subtle or unconscious form of sexual disturbance. Deborah's father taught at a conservative university. Secretly he led a life of duplicity and saw prostitutes. Though as a teen Deborah had no overt knowledge of her father's duplicity, unconsciously somehow she knew what he liked. She would dress on the edge—tastefully yet provocatively. She wore memorable cologne. And though married she became entwined in affairs. She more overtly became like the object of her father's secret passions. Was she somehow seeking her father's approval and attention? Her atypical hypersexuality emerged from a developmental disturbance.

Sheila, by contrast, simply grew up in a dysfunctional home and wanted out. She left home and found she could make money to survive and buy drugs by selling sex. Sheila was not hypersexual; she was just surviving and made some confused choices about how to survive.

For men sexual infidelity is the norm; relational infidelity is the variation. The intensity of relationship some men have with their work or recreational activities can become the functional equivalent of infidelity to their spouse and idolatry to God. We need not look far to identify how it manifests itself; it likely involves booze, business or balls.

Wes worked hard and suffered under great financial stress due to a significant loss of assets in some ill-timed business transactions. He felt that his wife demanded but was never satisfied with his help with the children. Wes wanted a break. Often late in the evening he would tell his wife he had to go back to work, but he would actually go to play pool. Five years later, Wes traded pool for a lover and, finally fed up with striving to keep everyone else happy, came out of the closet with his secret obsessions.

Sam worked hard during the day building his business empire in commercial real estate. On the way home he would purchase a six-pack and begin drinking, consuming it all within a couple hours. He hid whiskey in the garage, attempting to conceal the volume he actually consumed. It comforted him to think about, plan and execute his secret rendezvous. Sam had a relationship with alcohol. Over time this extramarital relationship replaced his wife.

Jeff liked to keep his business activity separate if not concealed from his wife. He obsessed on his investments, putting more and more money into highly speculative stocks. He had pledged to his wife to quit this pattern if his losses hit $10,000. With losses over $150,000 and savings rapidly depleting, however, he could no longer conceal this semi-secret, extramarital, intense relationship.

Business or recreation can be powerfully seductive, extramarital and intensely relational. Work can be complex and competitive and demand our attention. Relaxing a little, playing a round of golf with some friends, joining a softball league or going fishing can be legitimate but when taken to extremes or practiced in secret can nevertheless disrupt the balance in a marriage. When a man's wife refers to herself as a golf widow or to her husband's business as his mistress, the balance has been lost.

SUMMARY

While it helps to be able to type, define, classify and note the variations of infidelity, a more pressing question emerges. What causes infidelity? As we define the causes we get closer to knowing how to cure—or better yet, prevent—infidelity.

— 3 —

Causes of Affairs

What causes affairs? It's an important question. I've asked that question with more than a thousand couples. Knowing the cause does not heal the affair. But in an important way knowing why reframes the pain. If we know the cause perhaps we can prevent the recurrence for ourselves, and even the occurrence for others.

Collectively, after careful and thorough exploration, most couples identify the following factors:

- communication issues
- character development issues
- conflict resolution issues
- adult life stages or landmarks
- confused or broken choices

These factors conspire to create dysfunction in a marriage. And the dysfunction creates enormous pressure on the marriage. Often then this pressure gets expressed or acted out through infidelity.

Five years ago George ended an affair that had lasted three years. Along the way he and his wife, Mary, saw a couple of counselors but never succeeded at changing their marriage in a substantial way. Perhaps the counseling served to help them stay together and survive the trauma, but they were not thriving as a couple. They remained in a parallel relationship, miserable and merely polite in their marriage.

George rarely gets drunk, but during a party for soccer-league parents several people drank too much, including George. He made a pass at one of the mothers in attendance. The next day George and this woman exchanged suggestive e-mails and planned to rendezvous, but the e-mails were discovered by their spouses.

When we met to begin counseling, George wanted to get on with the work of changing the quality and nature of his relationship with Mary. He saw the soccer-party situation as a stupid error in judgment that he regretted and felt ashamed about. Mary viewed George's desire to move on into the future in a very different way. She was willing to accept the recent near miss as a drunken error in judgment reflecting the sickness of their marital state, but she felt that he had memorialized the prior three-year affair in his mind. George, she thought, was trying to control the process. Because they hadn't worked through the causes of the previous affair, Mary was left in a vacuum, at risk to imagine the worst.

A therapist who once worked for me says, "Understanding the events of the past is not necessarily curative but it does dignify the pain." With this backdrop let us explore the most frequent causes of affairs.

COMMUNICATION ISSUES

We live surrounded by a sea of communication. Even silence has a language of its own. Broadly all this communication could be categorized as either pure or polluted, balanced or imbalanced. And if we swim in polluted water we run the risk of becoming toxic ourselves.

What causes the water of words to become polluted and imbalanced? What causes poor communication?

Too much or too little focus on self or on others. People who place too much or too little focus on either themselves or others contribute to the pollution of communication. They tend to fall into one of several types: avoiders, competitives, placaters or compromisers.[1]

Avoiders do a poor job of empowering either themselves or others.

Avoiders at times appear passive or may avoid facing issues. Sometimes avoiders say to me, "We never fight. But our marriage is dead. And now we're thinking about divorce or something." Avoiders rationalize their behavior by assuming that if they can't effectively express their needs or frustrations, they're better off not bringing them up. However, even a poorly executed argument may have better results than avoiding issues altogether.

Competitives do a fair job of empowering themselves but a poor job of empowering others. Competitive people may appear aggressive or dominant. Alex complained a great deal about Debbie and often expressed anger toward her and others. Things in the marriage and family often went Alex's way at the expense of others. Other family members had to resort to secret subterfuge or be willing to be seen by Alex as openly defiant of him.

Placaters do a fair job of focusing on others but a poor job of empowering themselves. Placating people may appear accommodating or even self-sacrificing. Katie, Frank's wife, took care of everybody but herself. After several years of this Katie became depressed, fatigued and burned out.

Compromisers go through a process of making trades. They might say, "I'll give up on this if you give up on that." Both sides win and lose. Compromise might be seen as the practice of mutual dissatisfaction. Both sides force compromise that neither party finds fulfilling. Most legal divorces fall into this category.

A more constructive approach to relationships is collaboration. Collaborators do a good job of empowering both self and others. A collaborator might say, "First tell me what you think is important about this issue so I can understand your viewpoint, then I'll present what's important to me." I rarely encounter good collaborators.

Confused intersection management. Closely related to imbalanced relationships is the confusion of intersection management. People approach conversation differently. Competitive types tend to present their position to the exclusion of others. They may not realize when their turn should be over and fail to share the platform with others. By contrast, placaters may fail to assert themselves, creating a different problem. A placating spouse may swallow what they really want to say in order to avoid another encounter. Placaters sometimes report feeling like they are walking on eggshells.

Broken, negative or problem orientations. Poor communication also results from a broken, negative or problem orientation. Their communication tends to be critical rather than appreciative and encouraging. One researcher has discovered that high functioning couples maintain a ratio of five positive to every one negative interaction, whereas low functioning couples maintain a ratio of 1 positive to every 1.25 negative interaction.[2]

Lack of differentiation. Finally, poor communication results from a lack of differentiation between past experiences and present or future relationships. Naturally the experiences of our past form and influence our views, perceptions and responses in the present. They also combine to project into the future. When Gretchen casually asked Gene where he was going, Gene replied, "Do I have to tell you everything I'm doing?" Gene had perhaps failed to differentiate Gretchen (the present) from his invasive, domineering parents (the past).

Poor communication becomes a major factor contributing to the creation of conditions from which affairs germinate.

CHARACTER AND DEVELOPMENT ISSUES

Successful mountain climbing requires more than just good communciation. Certain character traits, such as caution or patience, are likewise critical. Conversely, the character traits of impatience or recklessness could prove disastrous. Similarly, flawed character (perhaps resulting from misguided or neglectful parenting, or perhaps due to some trauma) increases the likelihood of bad outcomes in the marital relationship.

What attracts an offending spouse to a third party often correlates with their criticisms of their partner. Interestingly, the offending spouse's developmental or family of origin issues usually correlate to the criticisms of their partner.

Hannah felt judged and neglected by her mother. She married Joe who originally gave her attention. But over time Joe seemingly became judging and neglectful—much like Hannah's mother. Finally Hannah bonded with a third party who met her need for acceptance and attention.

Hannah's criticisms of Joe correlated to her attraction to the third party. And Hannah's developmental or family of origin issues correlated to her criticisms of Joe.

Developmental issues play a role in causing infidelity. Certainly our past, the good and the bad of it, will impact our present and our future. And any need from the past will somehow express itself in the present. For example if you did not feel valued growing up, being valued in your adult relationships may become extremely important to you.

You can look at developmental issues in several ways. One of my favorites involves the idea that first we must attend to our need for security. After security has been resolved we can pursue significance. If you find yourself lost in the woods you must first attend to security issues: a plan, shelter, warmth or fire, water, food. Once you satisfy these survival needs you can consider other issues such as figuring out how to get rescued, keeping a journal or writing a letter to those you love.

Attachment and separation. In relationships security can be further subdivided into the needs for *attachment* and *separation*. Early on, a child has literally physical attachment and connection to the mother. Even after the child no longer has a physical connection (the cord is cut), attachment to the parent is still necessary for the child's very survival. As the child matures, however, separation becomes the expected and necessary next step. This cycle repeats itself several times over our life.

If you listen carefully to the core issues people identify in adult relationships, you can hear these themes presented. An adult with attachment issues might say things like

- I don't feel like I have a connection with you.
- We are not intimate.
- We don't share things anymore.
- It's like we are separate strangers.
- You are not giving me what I need. I need you.

Tricia (whom we met earlier) grew up feeling disconnected from her alcoholic parents. Now married, she wanted to make up for that. She'd say to Eric, "Can't you just look at me when we talk or sometimes hold my hand. I feel like if you really cared for me you would be giving me attention and be available for me." When Tricia started running with her neighbor, she got the intense connection she had yearned for. And eventually she had an affair.

An adult with separation issues might say things like

- I need space.
- You are smothering me.
- You are controlling me.
- I don't think you need to know everything I'm doing.
- I'd like to have some privacy and freedom.
- You can not catch me, control me or make me.

David came from an orthodox Greek family. He inherited sizable assets from a family trust. He wanted to please his parents. They had been good to him. His mother liked the woman he was dating, which influenced his decision to marry her though she was older than he was. As his children got into high school and college he became increasingly bored. Eventually he had an affair. He said, "All my life I've done everything for everybody else. I've been doing things for my mother, my wife, my kids and the company. I've never done anything just for myself. Well now I have."

Sometimes very immediate, surface factors can create the same pattern. Sylvia, a mother of three young children, had children literally hanging on her all day long. Her husband tried to arouse a sexual response at night in bed; Sylvia was exhausted and touched out, and told him, "Sorry—I need a break."

Identity and competence. In relationships significance can be further subdivided into the needs for *identity* and *competence.* Again this makes sense if you think of a developing child. A child experiments with several identities: an action hero, a fireman, a cowboy, a nurse, a homemaker, and so on. The child wants to play out these identities and have others interact with them in that role. As the child matures in time they become focused on competence: they brush their teeth, make their bed, tie their shoes, ride a bike, learn the alphabet. Again this cycle repeats itself several times over several years.

In adult relationships if you listen carefully to the core issues people identify you can hear these themes presented. An adult with identity issues might say things like

- I need to be recognized for who I am.
- I'm tired of doing the right thing for everybody else.
- You don't really care about me and what I think or want.
- I want someone who appreciates and accepts me.
- I'm tired of being ignored or taken advantage of.
- I was flattered that someone cared about and was attracted to me.
- I was desperate for someone to care about me and not put me down all the time or say that I never did anything right.

Alicia loved music, poetry and spiritual ideas. Her husband, an attorney working for a large bank, had other things on his mind. Eventually Alicia formed a relationship with a man who showed a keen interest in Alicia's interests. Alicia said, "I did not set out to find someone. But with my friend we talked and talked about so many passions we shared, then we kissed, and I opened up inside." They prayed together and exchanged poetry and eventually had an affair.

By contrast an adult with competence issues might say things like

- You don't appreciate what I do.
- This is something I must do or I won't feel fulfilled.
- I want to be recognized for what I've achieved or for what I'd like to achieve.
- I've worked hard and sacrificed to get to this point.

Mike worked as an international vice president of marketing. Competitive, charming and well versed in his field, he readily succeeded. He loved achieving. He reported having a perfect life: "I'm at the top of my field, I love my wife and two beautiful kids, now my wife is pregnant again. Everything is going my way." Then one night on a cruise with sales associates he had sex with a female coworker. Later he discovered that he'd contracted Herpes II in the process, which would put his wife's pregnancy or delivery at risk.

One author proposes that we, like developing trees, must go through four distinctive stages:

1. Survival (a seed sprouts into a sapling)
2. Stability (the sapling grows into a stable tree with a small diameter)
3. Success (the tree grows deep, firm roots, a strong trunk and a large canopy)
4. Significance (the mature tree reproduces an abundance of fruit and other successful trees)[3]

Another author simply proposes that we all have innate needs.

- affection
- sexual fulfillment
- conversation
- recreational companionship
- honesty and openness
- physical attractiveness
- financial support
- domestic support
- family commitment
- admiration

Those needs may vary due to our past development, our gender or present circumstances. When these needs fail to be met the couple move into the states of conflict and withdrawal. The risk of infidelity increases.[4]

Everything alive has needs. In part those needs result from how we developed. The neglected child may become the adult who cries out for attachment and connectedness. The smothered child may become the adult who demands separation, distance and some breathing space. The child not valued as an individual may become the adult who craves individual recognition and to be valued as a person. The child not recognized for their achievement may become the adult obsessed with success and accomplishment. The variations and permutations could go on and on and fill a library. In the final analysis, whether conscious or unconscious, the needs left over from childhood become magnets pulling one into infidelity.

CONFLICT RESOLUTION ISSUES

Poor communication coupled with deep unmet needs creates the perfect environment for conflict. The term "irreconcilable differences" has become popular as a justification for a dissolution or divorce. I take "irreconcilable differences" to generally mean that the parties simply have not been trained in conflict resolution.

Most people have never taken a course in conflict resolution. Somehow people believe that this skill must be instinctual. But instinct most likely inclines a person to fight back, give up or take flight. The skills involved in conflict resolution feel more counterintuitive. The assertive person must learn to be sensitive to others. The sensitive person must learn to be assertive.

More often than not conflicts deteriorate into win-lose situations. One party wins and the loser harbors resentment. In perhaps the best scenarios couples strive to compromise. However, in compromise often both parties lose something. Far better and more elegant solutions exist. Conflict, however, is inevitable, and unresolved conflict increases the risk of an affair—which itself, whether hidden or known, further adds to the intensity of the conflict.

ADULT LIFE STAGES OR LANDMARKS

Landmarks play a role in the unique timing of affairs. Affairs often occur at or near key points in time. These landmarks seem to pressurize the marital system. Landmarks signal a time of heightened vulnerability. They become crucial choice points.

The first three to five years of marriage is one such landmark. This time frame contains enormous change. You go from single life to married life. You become more fully immersed in a new extended family. Married partners literally go from honeymoon into reality. You experience more in depth the strengths and weaknesses of your partner and of yourself. A high number of affairs occur during this landmark transition.

Pregnancy and birth of a child is another landmark. During pregnancy and postdelivery couples become less sexually active due to sickness, discomfort, medical risk or the need to protect the fetus. And with birth the focus and resources of the family get allocated differently. The dependent child gets a big portion of finite resources: attention, energy, time and so forth. A high number of affairs occur during this landmark transition.

Infertility creates a different type of landmark. Going through treatment for infertility can turn lovemaking into a job. Self-esteem can be challenged due to the physical flaw contributing to the infertility. People yearn to feel sexually attractive, potent and esteemed. A high number of affairs occur during this landmark transition.

When people have been married for seven to ten years, they may ask, "Is this as good as it gets?" They may think or say, "I don't like who I'm with, who I am, or what I'm doing." At this landmark people become intense about their displeasure and often act out that displeasure. A high number of affairs occur during this landmark transition. The vast number of people survive this transition by working harder but not necessarily smarter.

During the mid-life crisis (generally around age forty or so) people revisit those issues in an intensified manner. They've energetically built a family and a career, then ten years later they run out of steam, and life is arguably half over. A high number of affairs occur during this landmark transition.

When the last child is leaving home, one encounters another landmark. How often I've heard, "I'm gonna stick it out for three more years till my youngest graduates, then I'm leaving." Providing financial and emotional security for children through high school by staying married usually indicates parental responsibility. Perhaps your relationship with the children makes the marriage somewhat bearable. But the idea of being married without the children at home would be unbearable as the marriage now stands. Around this landmark affairs frequently occur as a stop-gap to the empty marriage or perhaps literally as a way out of the marriage.

THE SAGA OF HEATHER

Heather and Greg depict this scenario. Heather, a chiropractor, got married in her twenties and had a child. But her husband abused her emotionally and physically. By age thirty she began an affair with a physician, Greg. Soon she left her first husband and married Greg. In a couple years they had a child too. They never got training on how to have a good marriage. Greg, though not abusive, tended to control her and acted needy at times. So ten years later (at age forty) she had another brief affair. Greg by this time ran a successful medical practice, which enabled her to pursue her personal interests. Life was comfortable, though marriage felt dull.

From age forty to fifty Heather focused on her kids, her chiropractic practice and her personal interests. By the time she turned fifty her youngest son had only a year left before graduating from high school, and her mother had recently died. She told Greg she wanted to end the marriage and seriously entertained yet another affair.

Look at the timeline:

Twenties	Thirties	Forties	Fifties
new marriage	first marriage affair	second marriage affair	affair risk
abusing spouse	new marriage	controlling spouse	son age 17
	controlling spouse		lost mother
	birth of son		

Heather's affairs or risk-points occurred at major life transitions cyclically spaced about seven to ten years apart—landmarks that signal a time of heightened vulnerability. They become crucial choice points, which takes us to our next topic.

CONFUSED OR BROKEN CHOICES

Broken choices cause affairs. The decision or choice to pursue an affair involves a conscious choice coupled with unconscious influencers. We have detailed the bulk of those unconscious influencers: (1) communication issues, (2) character development issues, (3) conflict resolution issues and (4) landmarks. These factors interplay to pressurize the marital system and make a person's vision myopic.

Myopia involves a narrowing of a person's vision, a lack of discernment of the long-range perspective or consequences. People narrow their focus and mostly just see the pleasure of the moment, the person who holds the promise of meeting a deep need, or a way to retaliate against a spouse. I hear phrases like "I don't fully know why I chose to do this" or "If I had it to do all over again I would not do it or at least I would not do it the way I went about doing it."

In the myopia of broken choices you only see what pulls you toward the affair or what pushes you away from your marital partner. You do not see the big picture.

Adam and Eve only "saw that the fruit of the tree was good for food and pleasing to the eye, and also desirable for gaining wisdom." They were at that moment unconscious of their nakedness. They were unconscious of the cost of being banned from the Garden of Eden, and they were unconscious of the other curses that would follow. Adam and Eve suffered from myopia and made a broken choice. So does the person who chooses to enter an affair.

GENETICS: A MULTIGENERATIONAL AFFAIR

Before concluding this chapter I must at least mention the role of genetics. Perhaps intertwined with genetics, the infidelity of a parent may predispose their adult children to repeat the cycle of infidelity.

One author and therapist discovered a surprising correlation: In nine out of ten cases, either the straying partner, his/her mate, or both partners had adulterous parents. Most often, patients are unaware of this fact until uncovered in therapy.[5]

The Bible alludes to this intergenerational effect:

> The LORD is slow to anger, abounding in love and forgiving sin and rebellion. Yet he does not leave the guilty unpunished; he

punishes the children for the sin of the fathers to the third and fourth generation. (Numbers 14:18)

Recently published studies of female twins in the United Kingdom shed interesting light on the role of genetics. Researchers evaluated 1,600 female twin pairs. They found that when one female twin engaged in infidelity, their twin had a 41 percent chance of doing the same. This compares to an average rate of infidelity for women of only 18 percent in most Western cultures. Further analysis revealed not definite but suggestive associations.[6]

So what does this mean? Though not decisive, genetics appears to play some role. Raw genetics apparently also contributes to the mix of influencers. Simplistically, some inherited genetic factors may double the risk of having an affair. Fortunately we still have the freedom and ability to make choices in the best interest of ourselves and others. Being aware of risk factors can enable us to take corrective measures. God, according to the Bible, does not discount genetics but will not abandon a person to them.

PRESSURE, EARTHQUAKES AND AFFAIRS

When pressure builds up between the subterranean tectonic plates it needs to be released. Earthquakes represent something good and necessary happening in a potentially dangerous and destructive manner. So it is with marriages. When marriages or relationships get pressurized, because we are both social and sexual in nature, an affair often becomes the natural though destructive release for that pressure.

One morning in 1999 we awakened to news that a 7.6 Riechter Scale earthquake had just occurred with an epicenter in Joshua Tree, California. Our oldest daughter, a wilderness educator at the time, just happened to be in Joshua Tree with a group of twenty teens. The quake knocked out the phone lines. We anxiously awaited word of their status. By mid afternoon we got a call—no deaths, no injuries, no significant damage. The quake actually made her dream about driving her truck over a bumpy road. After awakening she said, "Oh that must have been an earthquake." She checked the camp and went back to sleep.

The rock of Joshua Tree is monolithic granite. The structures often are tents. The ground is solid, the structures are safe. Something good and necessary, the release of enormous pressure, happened in a secure and nondestructive manner.

SUMMARY

Shane and Gloria, like many couples these days, got married in their early thirties. They soon had two children and simultaneously aggressively pursued their careers. Gloria started her own successful medical service business while Shane locked in with a national corporation that supplied raw materials to industry.

The sheer demands of early stage dual careers and early stage parenting took a toll, leaving little time for them as a couple. They survived for about seven years, then hovering around age forty the pressures intensified and Shane began an affair with a female corporate officer. Gloria discovered Shane's duplicity and they entered a crisis. Gloria struck Shane and shouted at him to leave. Shane spent the night with family members. Neither one slept. Gloria sobbed through the night; Shane's heart beat with an intensity he felt in his ears. The next day they contacted me asking if we could meet soon. We met later that day.

Part three of this book will detail how we systematically brought order to their crisis, and how order has come to other couples like them. For now I want to look at their situation in the context of the causes of the affair.

Communication. Both Shane and Gloria spoke their mind, but when push came to shove Shane tended to placate Gloria. Over time Shane saw little sense in the argument and simply avoided the situation. They had broken communication, and subterranean pressures intensified.

Character development. Since Gloria owned a business that brought in more than 50 percent of their income, and since she had the intent of building her business for them, she pressed Shane for support and concessions. Could he come home promptly or early from work so she could deal with a crisis or catch a flight? Over time Shane, though capable, charming and successful, said "I felt insignificant." Shane wrestled with personal identity. They failed to understand and address a crucial character development issue, and the pressures further intensified.

Conflict resolution. With flawed communication and unrecognized, unaddressed character development issues, true capacity for conflict resolution became nearly impossible. Conflict resolution functioned only at a superficial level—far from the substantial levels needed. Pressures groaned with intensity.

Landmarks. After seven or so years of this with no obvious or tangible change foreseeable in the future, Shane thought, *I'm trapped. I can't effect change and I can't get out. I'm over forty years old!* Pressures intensified to such an extent that structures began to melt, solid rock faulted and buckled.

Confused choices. Going with the flow of the forces at play was for Shane almost a nondecision. For a different outcome Shane would have had to somehow decide to resist the pressures firmly in place. His failure to do so, nevertheless, was still a personal decision—a confused choice.

Genetics. To top it off, Shane's father had an affair and left his mother. At minimum his father modeled a flawed approach to life's pressures. Maybe his father transferred genetic predisposition.

What a mess. And this is mild to moderate standard operational procedure. You can change the roles. You can change the details. But this scenario captures the primary causes of infidelity. Infidelity is about enormous pressures. Infidelity is about brokenness in the domains of communication, character development, conflict resolution, landmarks, choices and possibly even genetics. In fact, we are on an ascent into or through brokenness that follows a path through several stages, which we will next examine.

PART TWO

Ascent into Brokeness

— 4 —

Growing Up

Mountains are complex structures. Some parts of the mountain are stable, other parts unstable. Mountains even create their own weather by a process known as orographic lift. Fronts moving across a mountain get compressed into higher density as the air is displaced by the mountain itself and forced up.

People are complex structures too. Some parts are stable. Other parts are unstable. We are whole and broken. People even create their own weather or environment to some extent. Wherever Sam goes it rains. Susan is a ray of sunshine. The risk of infidelity, like the risk of an avalanche, occurs by nature in our very structure.

Taking a broad or panoramic view, infidelity involves stages or phases. The first three phases usually occur in childhood and early adulthood, before entering into marriage or a committed relationship:

- brokenness in the family of origin
- brokenness in the peer group
- brokenness in dating relationships[1]

BROKENNESS IN THE FAMILY OF ORIGIN

Long before you marry or commit to someone, the first family you know, your birth family, begins to shape you. Hopefully, most of your childhood involved whole experiences. You had sufficient food, clothing, shelter and healthcare to meet your physiological needs.

You experienced safety and received instruction on how to protect yourself and others. You had a sense of belonging to a family, and you felt loved. Your sense of self-esteem increased as you continued to develop and grew in competence. Eventually you became empowered to pursue a course in school and life that had meaning for you.

Inevitably, however, trauma occurs—you feel neglected or ignored, someone controls you, someone puts you down for something you value, or you fail to perform some task or develop some competency. More subtly, perhaps, you get constructed with some missing piece. Perhaps others taught you how to compete but less so how to demonstrate compassion—or just the reverse. In the end, no one is perfect. Our wholeness and brokenness shows up most clearly when interacting with others.

One personality inventory, the California Psychological Inventory (CPI), clearly lists thirty different dimensions of personality. The creators attempted to identify every conceivable theoretical aspect of personality without too much overlap.

CPI Scales
Each "scale" identifies a major personality trait.

1. Dominance	10. Self-control	19. Flexibility
2. Capacity for Status	11. Good Impression	20. Femininity/Masculinity
3. Sociability	12. Communality	21. Managerial Potential
4. Social Presence	13. Well-being	22. Work Orientation
5. Self-acceptance	14. Tolerance	23. Creative Temperament
6. Independence	15. Achievement via Conformance	24. Leadership
7. Empathy	16. Achievement via Independence	25. Amicability
8. Responsibility	17. Intellectual Efficiency	26. Law Enforcement Orientation
9. Socialization	18. Psychological-mindedness	27. Tough-mindedness

CPI Vectors
Several traits combine or interact to form more general or global "vectors" or tendencies.

1. Externality vs. Internality	2. Norm-Favoring vs. Norm-Doubting	3. Ego Integration

Never do two people score the same. The good and bad experiences of childhood push you to score high or low on these dimensions. They create unique needs, drives and reward systems that get acted out in the dynamics of your relationships—including your marital and infidelity relationships.[2]

THE SAGA OF RICHARD

Richard is a successful businessman who owns several prominent franchises. Having just concluded a three-month affair with his children's piano teacher, he described his feelings about his marriage before the affair as terribly alone and isolated. His wife, Robin, asked him to recall the first or most important time he'd had a similar feeling, and he began to sob. He immediately recalled being alone in the fourth grade and crying on the steps out in front of his house.

Richard's parents divorced when he was in the first grade. Due to family hardships Richard moved to Texas to live with his grandma in the third grade. Then he moved back home to New York in the fourth grade, where he was the new kid—the outsider. With no dad and no friends, he cried alone on the steps and then went on with life. When he was twenty-eight, his mother committed suicide. When he was thirty, his brother died of a drug overdose.

In various ways Richard was saying to his wife before he began the affair, "Love me, care for me, I am important too, include me." Robin admitted hearing his complaints of dissatisfaction but hadn't realized how serious they were. It might be argued that Richard's affair actually began in the fourth grade.

BROKENNESS IN THE PEER GROUP

The patterns of childhood and home relationships tend to get repeated with peers. A parent may dominate a child; that child will likely form relationships with dominating playmates. Why? The child knows the dance steps for survival with a dominating person. If a child functions in the alpha or dominant role at home, the same child will tend to be in the alpha role with peers.

Sometimes, but less often, the reverse happens. A child who gets suppressed by a parent at home may become the suppressor among peers. I call this a system reversal. But it's still the same dance: now the child emulates or becomes the parent when with peers.

The point is simple. Early patterns in one way or another get deeply reinforced with the next age appropriate social grouping. The preschool pattern once imprinted, the strengths and weaknesses, the deep needs and desires, usually gets reenacted throughout grade school and junior high with same sex peers. Around puberty the pattern tends to repeat itself with friends and partners of the other sex.

BROKENNESS IN DATING RELATIONSHIPS

My mother did a good job parenting me all things considered, but at times I overwhelmed her. I have very early childhood memories of her telling me to settle down and straighten up or she would leave me. That statement did not help me relax at all. So she would pretend to leave me by going out the back door of our home. She would slam the door behind her and lock it from the outside so I could not follow her. After I screamed a few minutes (which seemed like an eternity) and promised to be good, she returned.

While I fortunately matured into a well-rounded youth, I developed a narrow but certain hypersensitivity to threats of abandonment. I had two best male friends: Tim and Matt. At one point I took a trip with Tim and several older strangers. Tim naturally got quite involved with explorations that were part of the trip. He neglected me. How could he do that? Weren't we best friends?

Later in life I married Sharon. In our early marriage at times we argued with intensity. One day while arguing Sharon went up the stairs and slammed and locked the door between us. I didn't cry, but I yelled with an impassioned intensity about my need to talk to her right now. And I felt a sick dependency on her response.

I'm sure you see what happened. Both Tim and Sharon activated my hypersensitivity to abandonment. My solution involved attachment to someone. Later on I would learn about a very different solution involving God, but at the time I simply yearned for someone to stay connected with me during moments of interpersonal intensity. I had an unmet need.

SUMMARY

The inevitable family of origin dysfunction, followed by peer group dysfunction, followed by heterosexual dysfunction lays the seedbed for the future probability of infidelity. Genetics and the family of origin forge your personality and traits. Your personality and traits create unique needs, drives and reward systems that get acted out in the dynamics of subsequent relationships - most often first with same sex peers, then later in heterosexual relationships. By the time you marry, your system has an imbedded trap ready to draw you or your partner down the path toward infidelity. This book is about prevention, rescue and survival. Next we look at the phases of a typical marriage and see how this plays out.

Romantic Love

Romantic love involves bonding with another person. Several factors create attraction and lead to the experience of bonding. Research identifies three primary factors: similarity, proximity and reward.

SIMILARITY

Similarity occurs at two levels, the conscious and the unconscious. At a conscious level people get attracted to partners who bear broad, somewhat obvious similarities: race, ethnicity, faith, education, values, financial status, interests, attractiveness, activity level and so forth.

Conscious similarity plays an important role in attraction and bonding. Unconscious similarity, however, may play a more crucial role. We have already noted that your family of origin shaped you. You developed certain characteristics and traits, and assumed certain roles to adapt to that developmental experience. We might say you learned a dance of intimacy, and you learned to dance with a certain type of partner or partners, to lead or to follow. At an unconscious level one often gets attracted to a partner bearing characteristics similar to those in the family of origin.

My wife's father tended to dominate the family yet had admirable and inspiring goals. Though not as intense as my wife's father in his early years, I too had the characteristics of a dominant or strong man with inspiring goals. I expressed my dominance in more subtle ways, but I clearly resembled my wife's father. She knew how to live with a man like that.

Most people select a partner similar to themselves at a conscious level. But at an unconscious level they either pick, perceive or produce a partner similar to those in the family of origin.

If you grew up with controlling parents, even if your partner actually does not tend to be out of balance in respect to control, your hypersensitivity to issues of control make you inclined to *perceive* your partner as controlling. Therapists call this projection. Over time if you try to evade your partner's influence, you may *produce* or sculpt a controlling partner due to your evasion. This process destines you to feel blessed from the start but cursed over time.

One noteworthy exception bears mentioning: a system reversal sometimes occurs instead of a system match. Cynthia grew up on a mission field with rigidly religious parents. Eventually she rebelled. She had enough of that, so by the time she selected a partner she intentionally chose a mate who had lived wild and bold. Cynthia found him pleasurably exciting and fulfilling. But over time Cynthia tired of these characteristics and became more rigidly religious herself. At an unconscious level Cynthia bonded with a partner similar to herself, but over time in a system reversal she became more similar to her parents.

What about the common idea that opposites attract? Research does not confirm that opposites attract—quite the contrary, actually. Often at an unconscious level and early in a relationship we find complementary traits in our partner intriguing, appealing and attractive. For example, I'm publicly confident, rather systematic and patient. My wife is sensitively polite, correct and emotionally a rich palate. Early on I found myself drawn to her emotional intensity and sensitivity. But after a couple years of marriage my wife found me to be at times so confident as to be rude, so systematic as to be compulsive and so patient as to be slow. Meanwhile I found her to be so po-

lite and correct as to be hypersensitive and so emotional as to be ir-
rational.

We first get attracted to our partner's complementary traits, but
rather than add those traits to our own behavioral repertoire, we
wind up criticizing our partner for possessing them in abundance.
"Opposites attract" is not a sustainable basis for attraction.

PROXIMITY

Proximity—geographical access in space and time—creates attraction and offers a bonding experience. Research shows that you more
likely will be friends or friendly to your next-door neighbor than to
a neighbor five houses away.

Proximity comes from convenient access. A myriad of examples
could be presented: you and your partner are from the same school,
same town, same church or same office, or perhaps you have a common acquaintance.

We tend to become attracted to people proximal to us. Dating couples tend to spend lots of time together thus creating attraction. As
the relationship matures, however, the couple may spend less and
less time together; meanwhile, they often find more and more of their
time is spent with work associates. As they do so, many find themselves becoming more attracted to their coworker than to their
spouse.

REWARD

Reward also creates attraction and offers yet another bonding experience. At the most primitive behavioral level, reward draws the receiver toward the giver. By contrast, punishment pushes the receiver
either against or away from the giver. In the romantic phase of a relationship a couple tends to reward each other with regularity.

John Gottman, a marital researcher, has documented that high-
functioning couples reward one another at a ratio of about five posi-

tives for every one negative, whereas at-risk couples make about four positive comments for every five negative comments. Not only the ratio but the frequency of interaction tells a story as well. During a dinner hour, high-functioning couples will make a bid to connect about a hundred times in ten minutes. At-risk couples make a bid to connect only sixty-five times in ten minutes.[1]

Perceived acts of kindness—rewards—occurring in the midst of life-threatening circumstances can cause even a captive to bond with the captor. On August 23, 1973, three women and one man were taken hostage in one of the largest banks in Stockholm. They were held for six days by two ex-convicts who threatened their lives but also showed them kindness. To the world's surprise, all of the hostages strongly resisted the government's efforts to rescue them and were quite eager to defend their captors. Indeed, several months after the police saved the hostages, the hostages still had warm feelings for the men who threatened their lives. Two of the women eventually got engaged to their captors.[2]

The point is simple and profound. Reward brings people toward one another and inclines them to bond. Later on in a long-term relationship, people tend to take each other for granted, people stop being on their best behavior, and reward is replaced with criticism. At that point people become more vulnerable to reward that comes from others, and the risk of infidelity heightens.

CHARACTERISTICS OF THE ROMANTIC LOVE PHASE

Both conscious and unconscious similarity, proximity and reward combine to create attraction. Attraction then leads to the experience of romantic love. And the experience of romantic love has universal and unmistakable characteristics.

- *Idealization.* Idealization best characterizes the overall experience. The couple tends to primarily see the good in one another. The bad gets denied and/or remains carefully concealed. Each consistently strives to put forth their best impression.

- *Unconscious incompetence.* The lovers remain mostly unconscious of each other's incompetence.

- *Positive response.* The lovers move toward each other and engage in play, mating and nurturing.

- *Heightened sensory acuity.* The lovers see, smell, taste, hear and touch a richer palate. They are more conscious of their surroundings, and they attribute that consciousness positively to one another.

- *Oneness.* They may think or say, "I can't live without you."

- *Completion.* They may think or say, "You have made my life complete."

- *Familiarity and timelessness.* They may think or say, "It seems like we've always known each other and we've always been together."

Deeper levels of commitment, engagement and marriage often result. But the sense of timelessness, completion, oneness and idealization that propels people toward a lifelong commitment lasts around a year and a half—and most of the stages take place prior to the wedding!

SUMMARY

Similarity, both conscious and unconscious, proximity in time and space, and reward converge to create the uniquely powerful bonding experience called romantic love. Intoxicatingly intense, though relatively brief, romantic love forges a necessary and valuable bond between two individauls. The couple, unconscious of their incompetence, or perhaps overconfident in their competence, get married. Marriage feels like a great event—a grand processional.

The marriage day has for most people in America become the most complexly demanding and costly single day event in one's developmental journey. To marry, one ascends to a new elevation. But at higher elevations the air begins to thin, and many couples continue their ascent into brokenness.

— 6 —

Civil War

Over and over again I hear "I can't believe I married my father (or mother)." Or "I can't believe I'm becoming just like my father (or mother)." Frankly it makes a lot of sense when you think about it. We've experienced wholeness and brokenness in our families of origin and seen those traits reinforced in peer and romantic relationships. Shouldn't we expect the brokenness of the past to present itself again in our marriage?

THE SAGA OF LUKE AND DIANE

Luke ran a successful business. He worked too hard making it all happen and ultimately felt burned out. Diane stayed focused on mothering two young children and finishing up a graduate degree. When Luke came home he had the children thrust at him so Diane could fix dinner, study or take off to her internship obligations. Luke and Diane both drank to anesthetize the stress. When a few precious flexible moments arrived on weekends they'd pick at each other and verbally fight. Then one or both would be too negative or too tired to engage in any consistent sexual intimacy. Luke and Diane were in a civil war. This went on for months.

Luke had flashbacks to how his parents also fought, how his dad drank too much, threw himself into his work and barely had time for Luke growing up. And he remembered how his older brother always picked on him and put him down. Had he somehow married his father and brother in the form of his wife, or had he himself somehow become just like them?

A few weeks later after an office party, everyone drank too much, a coworker pursued him sexually, and Luke had a one night stand. The next day he was riveted by guilt; his stress level seemed to double.

The Saga of Linda and Lance

Linda said, "We rarely argue, but sometimes I wonder if life is worth living." Linda's father worked as a surgeon and had constantly pushed the children toward perfection and simply did not attend to her emotional needs.

Linda married Lance, who also practiced medicine. Lance spent his days listening to his patients' health and personal struggles. When he came home he wanted to escape the emotional drain of people. Though a sensitive man, Lance nourished his soul mostly through time alone. This, combined with the presence of an intense teenage son who stayed up late most nights, cut into any sense of private time with Lance for Linda.

In this environment Linda drank in the attention paid to her by a neighbor. Like her father he also was a surgeon. He complimented her beauty. They talked of matters of faith that meant so much to her. He fed her need for emotional connection and compliments. They had an affair that lasted about a year.

Finally Lance put the pieces together and confronted Linda. As Lance and Linda shared together in my office, Linda identified how she felt—frustrated, sad and lonely. She recalled a time when she was seven and her teacher asked the children to say "I love you" to somebody special to them. She picked her father, who replied, "You better be careful who you say that to." Her father missed a crucial moment to build esteem in his daughter and connection between them.

PRESENT, PAST AND FUTURE

We are always dealing with some dimension of time. We get triggered in the present, but our perception of the present has a history in our past. The past forms the databank that we routinely access in order to determine our present perceptions, decisions and actions. Harville Hendrix, in his book *Getting the Love You Want,* proposes that you select your partner because they match the image (or *imago*) that your unconscious constructed of your primary caregivers in an effort to heal or finish childhood. It could be argued that the civil war in marriage relationships springs from the past trying to somehow resolve itself in the present.

Even if an imago match did not occur, two other conditions make the past inescapable.

Projection. Some people perceive their partner as resembling negative people in their past, even if their partner does not have those traits. This is called projection. If someone had a controlling parent, it could make them hypersensitive to any hint of control by their marriage partner. So the innocent question "Where are you going?" gets perceived as controlling behavior.

Re-creation. Another group of people actually re-creates the past by their own actions. The role they take in relationships influences others to react in predictable ways. Victor's parents refused to let him get a car when he turned sixteen, so he secretly purchased one and parked it two blocks away from his house. In marriage he continued a pattern of highly secretive behavior, including infidelity. Over time his wife reacted to his secretive behavior by becoming more controlling.

Pattern reversal. Some people consciously or unconsciously reverse the pattern. Rachel's parents were strict, so Rachel consciously decided to marry somebody who was free, even wild. In fact she made an overcorrection and over time came to detest her partner's wild tendencies. Over time she became more like her strict parents toward her marriage partner. This system reversal occurs less frequently but does occur.

The past remains inescapable. We must consciously deal with it or it will dictate a lot of what we do.

INTERNAL SYMPTOMS VERSUS EXTERNAL SYMPTOMS

People tend to react to the civil war in one of two broad ways. Some internalize the struggle. In clinical terms such people are more likely to develop some form of neurosis. They may become depressed or anxious, or more prone to illness through the suppression of their immune system. They possess more defensive or passive features.

By contrast, some tend to externalize the struggle. In clinical terms such people are more likely to exhibit some form of personality disorder. They may blame others and express anger and rage. They possess more offensive or active features.

The civil war tends to make you either a victim or a victimizer, or both. Various permutations of these possibilities create different predictable outcomes. Two external (aggressive) partners create a more combatant relationship. Two internal (passive) partners create a more peaceful though still unfulfilling relationship. The most frequent pattern, however, seems to be that of one partner mostly dominating and the other partner mostly submitting.

The experience of civil war has universal and unmistakable characteristics.

- *Awfulization.* Awfulization best characterizes the overall experience. The warring pair tend to primarily see the bad in the other. The good is denied or remains carefully ignored. Each becomes at risk to fall into a pattern of being at their worst.

- *Consciousness of incompetence.* The couple become mostly conscious of each other's incompetence.

- *Negative response.* The couple move either against or away from each other, engaging in classic fight or flight.

- *Depressed sensory acuity.* The couple's senses are diminished, and they attribute the lack of acuity to a lifelessness in their relationship.

- *Separation.* They may think or say, "I can't stand to live with you."

- *Incompletion.* They may think or say, "Something is missing."

- *Unfamiliarity and disbelief.* They may think or say, "I'm in the wrong place with the wrong person. How did I ever get here?"

A shallow connection leads to a parallel marriage; dissolution or divorce often result. Many people nowadays seem to have a low tolerance for marital suffering or suffering in general. We demand more and put up with less. Don't throw in the towel too quickly, though. Research indicates that over half of at-risk couples will significantly improve within five years. Transformation, more likely than not, is within your reach.

CHOICE

Molly sat on my sofa and said, "I'm so confused. Part of me wants to be a loving wife, and the other part of me just wants to run away and be alone or with someone who treats me right. Right now Sam makes me sick, and the children overwhelm me."

The civil war becomes a time of hard choices and raw reactions without much conscious deliberation. Sometimes an internal conversation goes on, a demon on one shoulder and an angel on the other. The angel says, "Keep your vows, remain faithful, and work things out." The demon argues back, "You've already tried that for several years; where has it gotten you? Do what you feel like doing for once in your life." In other situations there's not much thinking to it. Over time our brains get programmed with automatic responses to stressful situations. We get programmed for some form of fight (action against the other) or flight (action away from the other). Out of Molly's resentment she makes a critical comment to Sam, "It would help if you spent more time around here helping me with the kids instead of always being preoccupied with work." Sam (without conscious thought or deliberation) instantly reacts with sarcasm, "And you make it awfully pleasant to be around here!"

WHOLE, BROKEN, WHOLE

Going through cycles of wholeness and brokenness might be considered a universal phenomenon. One day we are healthy (whole), the next few days we are miserably sick with the influenza (broken), then we get healthy again (whole)—if we don't die while we're sick! Business looks good and booms (whole). Then a key employee leaves and joins the competition, or the national economy takes a downturn (broken). The business survives and matures, and the national economy pick up (whole).

So it is with marriage. In the early stage of courting or marriage, couples experience a transient sense of wholeness, a sense of completion and elation. Those are the days of *unconscious incompetence*. In reality both whole and broken components reside in each of the two persons who make up the couple.

The civil war shifts the balance in a couple. The scales fall from their eyes and they begin to see—to their shock, dismay or disappointment—the broken. They become *conscious of incompetence* existing in themselves or their partner.

If the couple have the good fortune or means to find good training or models, even in a still largely broken or negative atmosphere, they can experience moments of *conscious competence*. But doing so requires effort. It is not yet natural. Their natural tendencies remain more broken than whole.

Fortunately some couples consciously practice the competent long enough for it to become mostly instinctual. Such individuals and couples experience *unconscious competence*. Marriage researcher John Gottman refers to them as "master couples."

Summary

The most complex machine in the world, I hear, is the space shuttle. Enormous effort went into designing a flawless mechanical system with redundant safeguards. But on February 1, 2003, it exploded during reentry over Texas. We became conscious of incompetence in the structure; the heat shield failed, and precious loved ones and heroes perished. It was broken, and had been for a long time.

Most everything has imbedded flaws. And sooner or later the flaws will emerge to impair or destroy the system. The bad news: every one of us also has imbedded flaws. Perhaps after reading this section you feel doomed and pessimistic. But if we accept the reality of brokenness we avoid wasting a lot of time and energy on blaming others and ourselves, and instead we can consider how to *heal* or even *prevent* structural breakdowns such as infidelity from occurring. In reading this book you are preparing to rescue someone (perhaps yourself) from the ascent into brokenness that so often reveals itself in infidelity. Rescue work can be challenging, draining and at times gruesome, but if we press on we may find it ultimately exhilarating and fulfilling.

— 7 —

The Evolution of Affair Conditions

Aaron and Christy had a good marriage for years. Then the last two years went bad. Aaron literally cried about how unhappy and lonely he felt. His wife listened and began making adjustments to address her part of his issues. But help came too little and too late. Perhaps due to impatience or desperation Aaron initiated an affair with their domestic assistant.

Usually some time during a marital civil war, conditions evolve to make you particularly vulnerable to—and ready—for an affair. It is almost as if you are being pushed. On the other hand, research shows that about 40 percent of the time affairs occur after someone is "pulled" toward a relationship, away from a marriage classified as at least OK.[1]

What message should we get from this? People in bad marriages certainly risk having affairs. But people in good-to-OK marriages risk having affairs too. Let's review this push and pull phenomena in more depth.

SIXTY-PERCENT PUSH

A negative marital environment can push you out the door. In chapter three I detailed the primary factors that push a person toward infidelity. The majority of affairs feature one or more of these factors:

- communication issues
- character or developmental issues
- conflict resolution issues
- adult life stages or landmarks
- confused or broken choices

Communication issues. Poor communication pushes you out the door because you and your partner are not experiencing reciprocal understanding. Conversations become uncomfortably imbalanced. One party consistently dominates the other, or both try constantly and simultaneously to dominate each other, or both in desperation give up even trying to communicate. The content of communication becomes more and more negative. The bad events of the past get dragged into the present and also cast a dark shadow on the future.

Character or developmental issues. Developmental issues push you out the door because deep underlying needs remain unmet. You or your partner yearn for security (a sense of attachment or connection, and by contrast, separation or simple freedom) and for significance (a sense of personal identity and competency).

Conflict resolution issues. Poor conflict resolution skills push you out the door because you instinctively prefer closure. The failure to resolve conflicts permits multiple issues to accumulate. In time it can seem to reach overwhelming proportions. This dramatically adds pressure to the already strained relationship.

Adult life stages or landmarks. Adult life stages or landmarks push you out the door because they create additional pressure or destabilization. Imagine the classic mid-life crisis. The last child has started high school. The next eight years become very clear. Work hard for four years. Then be ready to keep it up another four years to pay for college or go into more debt. Someone going through this passage may experience an urgency to achieve or experience something that they fear they will miss if they don't seize the moment and make a change. The situation, the stage, the landmark pushes one.

Confused or broken choices. Broken or confused choices push you out the door because they only aggravate an already confusing situation. Often couples can't fully identify with accuracy why things are bad, much less what to do about them except get away somehow. Like a fog settling in, guidance and navigational systems become impaired, and people make bad choices. They become more and more lost.

Multiple factors come together to literally push someone toward an affair. They want to get away from what they experience as negative, confusing, chronic and likely not solvable.

FORTY-PERCENT PULL

By contrast, approximately 40 percent of affairs occur when marriage relationships appear positive or neutral in nature. Infidelity researcher Shirley Glass found that over half of the men and a third of the women who had had affairs said they were happy with their spouses.[2] So what happens?

Simple attraction and confusion about boundaries play a big role. In chapter five I discussed the factors that create attraction—proximity, similarity and reward. A good-to-OK marriage can fall prey to another, newly attractive relationship.

Women and men today labor side by side in most working environments. Coworkers may spend more conscious hours with each other than with their spouses. They may share other similarities—they're both parents, for example, or they enjoy common recreational interests. If they are kind or sensitive to one another, this can come off as reward. Conditions become favorable for attraction to occur.

What do you do when you're attracted to someone? You likely spend even more time with them—talking, sharing innuendoes and laughing together at humorous situations. Often coworkers gradually take more risks with each other and communicate at ever-deepening levels. Conversations may turn from the world of work to personal issues, feelings, desires and dreams. Boundaries can get confused, blurred and knowingly or unknowingly violated. Once coworkers cross the line into this level of intimacy, affairs become a potential next step for deepening the relationship.

To make things more complicated, some people intentionally use their sexuality to acquire, secure or advance their positions at work. One of my daughters told me the story of a female coworker who rapidly rose to a position of prominence in her company because of a strategic affair with a coworker.

There are rewards in infidelity. Since we are social *and* sexual be-ings, positive relationships and sex by their very nature serve as pow-erful incentives. The perceived rewards of infidelity pull you to it even as incalculably higher costs lie hidden.

THE WRONG WAY TO HANDLE THE EVOLUTION OF AFFAIR CONDITIONS

Both pushing and pulling forces can occur simultaneously. Negative forces in the marriage can push you away. At the same time the pos-itive forces in another relationship can pull you toward it. This cre-ates a very powerful current that few can swim against. In fact you may not be able to effectively swim against a strong current; it would excessively tire you. Some of the ways that people try to resist this current actually add to the pressure.

Toying with the possibility of having an affair. Every year people who have no intention of doing so fall into the Grand Canyon. They get too close to the edge, overestimate their ability, underestimate the risk and lose their balance. In marital relationships, some people re-sort to fantasy as a release of the pressure they feel, but this ideation can actually encourage actualization—a person starts to believe in the potential of the fantasy relationship.

Acting out (without talking about) your negative thoughts and emotions.

Talking about these issues can be scary, but not talking about them can be much worse. It's easier to repair words than actions.

Blaming yourself or your partner. There is some value in taking responsibility for your part of a problem. But assigning blame tends to distract people from looking for a constructive solution.

Getting bad advice. Talking to friends, family members, coworkers, affair partners, volunteer or even professional counselors without specialized training in marriage or relationships often yields bad advice. Too often, though they mean well, they give advice that further complicates the problem or delays appropriate solutions.

Triangulation or substitute triangulation. Triangulation occurs when you focus more on the third party than on the relationship between you and your spouse. Substitute triangulation occurs when you substitute some other, perhaps addictive, focus (such as drugs, food, shopping, children) for the third party.

Focusing on the third party rather than your core values and commitments. The more you admire the third party or compare them to your spouse, the more confused you will become. Conversely, the more you focus on your core commitments and values—the marriage covenant or your marriage vows, for example—the better equipped you are to stay resolute in your marital relationship.

Waiting for a crisis. Most people come to see me after an affair has occurred. In fact I became convinced to write this book because most people wait until they find themselves in the crisis of infidelity before doing something about their marriage. There are ways of anticipating and ameliorating the affair conditions before they escalate, and the sooner you address those conditions, the more likely you are to avoid disaster.

THE RIGHT WAY TO HANDLE THE EVOLUTION OF AFFAIR CONDITIONS

You may struggle to resist the combined push and pull that threatens your marriage. But you can escape. Experts in survival advise us to swim at a right angle to the direction of a powerful current. There is a functional equivalent to this in relationships.

Commit to finding a way to create a strong marriage. Step away from the edge and look for the safe path. Treat your thoughts about infidelity as a signal that your marriage needs attention.

Talk about your inner struggle. Ultimately your spouse and you most need to talk. But sometimes spouses may not comprehend the seriousness of your inner struggle. They may not be tuned in yet or able to talk. In that case start by talking to friends, family and mentors who have successful relationships. Talk to those whom you can trust who have at the core the best interest of you and your spouse, as well as your family. If you don't have such a person in your life, find one.

Shirley Glass refers to such people as "friends of the marriage." They reinforce the value of marriage. Whereas bad advice weakens or confuses the marital bond, "friends of the marriage" demonstrate the ability to create problem-solving approaches that increase the strength of the marital bond.[3]

Replace blame with understanding. Without assigning blame, seek to understand how the situation evolved. Take responsibility for your part of or contribution to the problem. Whether your partner follows your model or not, work at being understanding of them.

Get professional guidance that specializes in marriage or relationships. It is hard for couples to get out of their old patterns without direct and live coaching. The best outcomes in relationships consistently come from learning and applying skills such as those for communication and conflict resolution. Get to know your counselor's model for work with couples, percentage of success in couples' counseling and philosophy about marriage.[4] A seasoned, neutral counselor often proves invaluable in getting a marriage back on track.

Embrace the usefulness of suffering, and choose optimism. Suffering together can be a bonding experience. To this day I vividly remember how my wife comforted me with a touch when I learned that my father had suffered a heart attack that would eventually prove fatal. Research has shown that those who comfort one another in the midst of pain may bond more deeply and experience a unique and powerful form of attraction. Identify how to best comfort the suffering. Choose to be optimistic about the eventual outcome.

Focus on the primary couple, the husband and wife. Even if it feels negative and counterproductive at first, your focus and energy belongs on you and the relationship you have with your spouse. Be aware of the tendency to triangulate, and take steps to redirect your focus.

Focus on your core values and commitments. As long as you look mostly at others, you will likely be confused or make poor decisions. You need to define your own core values and commitments. They will best guide you.

Be proactive, preventive and preemptive. When conditions for an affair have evolved, take action. Recognize that you are approaching or have entered a crisis situation; get help and make adjustments accordingly. If you do not do this, you risk a real, complex crisis that won't go away easily.

Master essential disciplines. I detail five essential disciplines in part three of this book. These practices help you to navigate relationships and prevent or overcome infidelity.

THE ROLE OF THE SUPERNATURAL

One day while I was in graduate school at Ohio State University, I thought *I would not have an extramarital affair, but if I did it would be with this kind of a person.* I detailed this person in my mind—how she would look, her character traits and what activities would appeal to her. To my shock, within five minutes I met a student while buying books at the bookstore who exactly met these criteria. She majored in creative dance. I felt like someone read my mind and created a perfectly programmed response.

The event felt surrealistic—simultaneously alluring and frightening. It also felt spiritual or supernatural, maybe even remotely evil. Was this a moment of temptation, some unusual psychological phenomena or mere coincidence?

Has this or something similar ever happened to you? Regardless of the nature of your experiences, I want you to seriously consider the role of the supernatural in the evolution of affair conditions. Many movies have been made about the battle between the forces of good and evil. Perhaps the forces of good and evil stand poised to do battle in your life over infidelity. What else looks so seductively enticing yet often converts into such a field of agonizing devastation?

Will you initiate or reciprocate an invitation to pursue an affair? If your partner levels with you about their serious inner struggles, will you understand and seriously engage change, or will you freak out and add to the pressure? When the evolution of affair conditions occurs you face a moment of truth—a choice.

THE JOY OF ENCOUNTERING SOMEONE STRONG AND WISE WHEN YOU ARE WEAK AND STUPID

At a critically pressured point in my marriage I asked my secretary to be more than just a friend. Wisely she responded that if we happened to form a deep relationship, that would change everything. Her simple yet profound reply saved me. She gave me a great gift. I'm indebted to her for that.

Several years later a female coworker basically asked me have an affair with her. This became my first opportunity to repay that earlier favor. I said, "I'm flattered, but if we happened to form a deep relationship, that would change everything." I also said, "I know that your invitation says something else. Perhaps it means you respect me and are frustrated with some aspects of your marriage. Perhaps it means that you are spiritually empty now. I believe in you, and I know you will figure out what it means and do the proper thing to make it right." And she did.

Conditions tend to evolve for an affair to occur. About 60 percent of the time this feels like being pushed; about 40 percent of the time it feels more like being pulled toward someone else. Sometimes both pushing and pulling occur simultaneously. But marriages experience these forces in an episodic way, as bad times come and go.

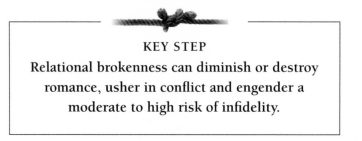

KEY STEP

Relational brokenness can diminish or destroy romance, usher in conflict and engender a moderate to high risk of infidelity.

Wrong ways and right ways exist to combat the evolution of these conditions. For you this may be a spiritual battle and journey. You have already climbed a good part of the mountain. You have ascended to a higher altitude. Oxygen is growing thinner and thinner. You struggle to breathe.

The farther you've gone in the evolution of affair conditions, the more fragile you become. A myriad of forces both push you forward and pull you toward the summit. Without some kind of intervention, you could very easily enter what climbers refer to as the death zone.

— 8 —

The Active Affair

The effects of an active but hidden affair on a marriage run the gamut from imperceptible change to glaring problems. Upon disclosure of infidelity, some offended spouses say, "I never imagined. I had no clue." But most say, "Something had changed. I knew it all the time."

There's a website promoting infidelity that provides tips for pulling off an affair without detection. The site emphasizes the importance of making no visible changes. It takes enormous amounts of planning, practice and focused concentration to make no changes, because with the initiation of an active affair huge changes occur.

EFFECTS ON THE OFFENDING SPOUSE

An addict recalls the rush of the last high and plans for the next. For the offending spouse, powerful forces create a mixture of romantic love, bonding, attraction or infatuation. Physiological and psychological forces rivet their attention on the third party or the overall situation. The offending spouse mostly experiences positive emotions such as excitement, negative emotions such as guilt or mixtures involving both excitement and guilt.

When interviewing clients, I like to ask what they find themselves thinking about during the course of the day. If alone in an interview, an offending spouse primarily mentions their preoccupation with thoughts about a third party. Secondarily they mention necessary survival thoughts regarding work or family obligations.

The offending spouse begins to dramatically experience what is called in behavioral psychology an "approach avoidance conflict." The subject simultaneously gets pulled toward and repelled by some situation. In experiments with rats, for example, this is tested by placing a reward (such as food) and a punishment (such as a mild electrical shock) at the end of a maze. The closer the rat gets to the reward the more they must endure an increasing electrical shock. The rat has mixed motivations. The rat wants the reward but not the punishment. Similarly the offending spouse wants the rewards of the affair (sex, romance, meaning, connection, friendship, excitement, etc.) but not the consequences (guilt, preoccupation, juggling, risk, etc.). The offending spouse gets drawn toward the rewards but repelled by the cost.

EFFECTS ON THE OFFENDED SPOUSE

Usually the offended spouse senses something different during an active affair. Depending on the nature of the change, the offended spouse may welcome or resent the change. The offended spouse, and basically all people for that matter, when negatively triggered will express or act out their feelings in one of three ways:

- Toward (connect or bond)
- Away (flight)
- Against (fight)

Which response emerges depends on the personality of the offended spouse and the nature of the situation. If the offended spouse wants more connection and the offending spouse pulls away due to the active affair, the offended spouse reacts negatively by increasing their efforts *toward* their partner, taking *flight* as a protective counter move or creating a *fight*.

Some people say, "During the affair we seemed to get along much worse." Others, however, may say, "During the affair we seemed to get along better." Even though a couple may get along better, the underlying structure of the marriage remains unstable or will become unstable shortly.

Undermining occurs when the support structure for the marriage erodes. For example, someone in an affair may look to the third party for advice or support rather than their spouse. This causes erosion and in time the visible structure, the marriage, sinks into a hole.

Renewed commitment occurs when, perhaps out of guilt, the offending spouse determines to try harder in the marriage. It's hard to maintain our renewed commitment to sobriety or dieting, however, when we continue to keep the refrigerator stocked with cold beer or ice cream. Renewed commitment on the part of the offending spouse usually has a short life due to the overall confusion, secrecy and lack of new tools to change the marriage process.

Temporary tension reduction occurs when the affair is treated as a helpful outlet for the tensions associated with problems in the marriage. The offending spouse may think, *We no longer fight about my need for relationship or sexual intimacy because I'm just getting that need met elsewhere.* This sounds like someone saying, "The financial pressure is off because my high-interest credit card gave me a cash advance."

Long-term polarization may be the most obvious effect. Polarization occurs when a person glamorizes the positive features of a third party and awfulizes the negative features of their spouse. The third party may become the embodiment of the good and the offended spouse may become the embodiment of the bad. Offending spouses may say things like "I don't know what I ever saw in you in the first place." "You are making me do this." Or "My affair partner has all I've ever longed for and more." Life is harsh and extreme at the poles.

Effects on Both Spouses

Researchers have identified an exhaustive list of effects, changes or cues resulting from sexual or emotional infidelity.[1] Interestingly men more quickly pick up on cues of their partner's sexual infidelity, and women more quickly pick up on cues of their partner's emotional infidelity.

Cues to Sexual Infidelity

- *His eating habits suddenly change.*
- *He sleeps more than he used to.*
- *She talks about sex more often.*
- *She is unusually upset when you do not want to have sex.*
- *He says "I love you" more frequently than he used to.*
- *He suddenly begins complaining of pain in his genitals.*
- *She acts more interested in having sex with you.*
- *She acts unusually happy when she is with you.*
- *He suddenly tries new and unusual positions during sex.*
- *He starts acting overly affectionate toward you.*
- *She is less sexually adventurous.*
- *Her clothing style suddenly changes.*
- *He has an orgasm less frequently during sex.*
- *He has unusual difficulty remaining sexually aroused during sex.*
- *She has unusual difficulty becoming sexually aroused.*
- *She goes through the motions during sex.*
- *He wants to have sex for a shorter duration than usual.*
- *He more often says you are doing something wrong during sex.*
- *She seems bored when you have sex.*
- *She suddenly refuses to have sex with you.*
- *He smells like he recently had sex—although not with you.*
- *He no longer wants your relationship to be exclusive.*

Cues to Emotional Infidelity

- *He starts asking you if you still feel the same love for him.*
- *He is unusually apologetic toward you.*
- *She doesn't want to go out on dates with you as often.*
- *She tells you less often that she enjoys spending time with you.*
- *He less often invites you to spend time with him and his family or friends.*
- *He acts unusually angry when you are together.*
- *She starts forgetting your anniversaries and other special dates.*
- *She does not say "I love you" as often as she used to.*
- *He is suddenly less forgiving when you make mistakes.*
- *He is unusually critical.*
- *She starts looking for reasons to start arguments with you.*
- *She starts acting rudely toward you.*
- *He becomes less gentle during sex.*
- *He doesn't respond when you tell him that you love him.*
- *She stops returning your phone calls.*
- *She acts unusually guilty after sex.*
- *You notice excitement in his voice when he talks about another woman.*
- *He acts nervous when a certain woman's name comes up in conversations with you.*
- *She doesn't look you in the eyes anymore.*
- *She starts talking to you about ending your relationship.*
- *He tells you that he does not love you anymore.*

EFFECTS ON THE THIRD PARTY

The third party most likely will be a friend or coworker. Remember that attraction results in part from proximity: working in the same office, frequenting the same gym or church, or living in the same neighborhood. Somehow the third party and the offending spouse interact frequently. The effect of the active affair on the third party before disclosure falls into two broad stages: "I am the special one" or "I am not special."

"I am the special one." The third party may think, *Of all the possible partners, he/she chose me.* This can make one feel special, honored and uniquely desirable. Even people with low self-esteem may feel special at this time.

Francine managed a recreation center in the suburbs. The recreations department supervisor saw her frequently during the peak summer season. Francine had a particularly poor self-concept. She did not like how she looked. But Francine's supervisor made overtures toward her and complimented her. Eventually they had a summer affair. "I couldn't believe that he found me attractive," she said. "He made me feel special."

"I am not special." Often affairs end because one or both parties refuse to make the next level of commitment. Francine's affair with her supervisor ended abruptly in the fall. Perhaps it ended because the peak season concluded and the two parties saw one another less frequently. Whatever the cause, Francine now faced the bitter possibility "Maybe I'm not really that special after all."

Another third party, Veronica, always celebrated special events such as birthdays and holidays out of town with the offending spouse. Over time she grew resentful. "He always celebrates special events with his wife in town. But he will only celebrate special events with me out of town." The failure to risk more, experience more, commit more over time leaves the third party not feeling special at all.

During World War II my eighth grade teacher was about to give a piece of chocolate to a German child when the child's mother stopped him. "Please don't give my child chocolate," she said. "After you leave I will have no more chocolate to give for a long time, and that will make my child very sad." The sweetness of an affair, such as it is, goes away. The third party awakens to hunger and emptiness—the sweetness turns bitter.

SECRECY GRID

Through the public ceremony of marriage everyone knows where the secrets, the intimacy, resides—with the married couple. The protective boundaries are clear, well defined, safely vaulted and insured. With infidelity only perhaps two people know about the shift of resources; the boundaries are vulnerable and at risk in multiple ways.

What I call the secrecy grid provides a dramatic way to understand the enormous effects of an active affair before disclosure. To simplify this, let's create a code:

A = the offending spouse
B = the offended spouse
C = the third party
v = secrets or intimate knowledge or confiding
x = no knowledge of secrets or intimate knowledge or confiding

A marriage prior to an active affair could be represented as

A (v), B (v), C (x)

The husband and wife share the secrets, the intimate knowledge of the relationship, and in all likelihood no one else knows what they know. They are "naked" with one another, and their intimacy holds "no shame" (Genesis 2:25).

A marriage after the start of an active affair could be represented as

A (v), B (x), C (v)

The offending spouse and the third party now share secrets and intimate knowledge, and in all likelihood no one else knows what they know. A lot of obsessing and yearning goes on. In order to maintain the secrets, the offending spouse and the third party make secrecy covenants. "No one will ever be told. No one needs to know but us."

SUMMARY

The active affair can be characterized as the final ascent into brokenness. When a mountain-climbing party summits and reaches the top of the peak, victory such as it is often has an incredibly short life—minutes, to be precise. The tired and oxygen-deprived party may be battling wounds and illnesses which resist healing. Their focus shifts to the costs of the ascent, the risks facing them in the current situation and preoccupation with survival. Higher elevations rightly deserve their nickname—the death zone. Active affairs occur in the death zone.

Ascent into Brokenness
Summary

If you put your mind to it, you could detail your successes and your positive traits, and it would be a long list—likely much longer than your failures or your negative traits. So what goes wrong? Brokenness, no matter how small, has the capacity to destroy or impair wholeness. A one-cent nail in a $50 tire stops and renders functionally useless a $30,000 automobile. A climber, fit and skilled enough to scale a tall mountain, risks injury or death due to one simple misstep.

Part two of this book has examined the ascent into brokenness. We explored repeating patterns of brokenness resulting from

- brokenness in the family of origin
- brokenness in the peer group
- brokenness in dating relationships

We explored how this pattern of brokenness gets intertwined with the selection of a mate and the common phenomena of

- romantic love
- civil war
- the evolution of affair conditions

We explored the further pressurization of brokenness and risk via

- communication issues

- character or developmental issues
- conflict resolution issues
- adult life stages or landmarks
- confused and broken choices

Brokenness peaks with the active affair. This leads us to a key step:

KEY STEP
Everybody is both whole and broken.
Brokenness can diminish or destroy romance,
usher in conflict and engender a
moderate to high risk of infidelity.

Part three of this book details essential disciplines for healing and, better yet, preventing infidelity. So whether you want to recover, avoid a tragic incident or help others on their journey through the mountains of life, the next section will give you a clear path and hope.

Descent into Wholeness

— 9 —

The Revelation

Sharing the Truth with Your Spouse

Focus: Communication
Goal: To Understand and Be Understood
Process: Take Turns as Presenter and Empowerer
Key Essential Discipline: SHARE

Many climbers say descending a mountain poses more risks than climbing. Climbing comes naturally; a mental charge accompanies the ascent. Descending, though necessary and sometimes urgently critical, may feel tedious, boring and anticlimactic, and produces a unique exhaustion. Climbers often begin their descent when they're tired and spent, with minimal supplies and damaged gear. It invites a special type of recklessness. My eldest daughter puts it this way: "It's hard or harder going down. You are tired and anxious to get back down. The excitement goes away. Sometimes the obstacles that come up irritate you. You feel like you are done."

This to me captures the mental challenge of the offending spouse. For sanity to return to the offending spouse, revelation of the affair becomes the first order of business. It involves humbling oneself and simply disclosing reality to the offended spouse. Though it may seem counterintuitive, this revelation creates the path for descending into wholeness, where you can breathe easier, and your wounds and illnesses can heal. The revelation is the path for the descent into wholeness. "To be born again," Salman Rushdie once wrote, "first you have to die."

I can never anticipate the outcome of working with the two or three parties involved in infidelity. There are factors hinting at success or failure of a relationship that can be identified. The odds may be ten to one that the marriage will succeed or ten to one that it will fail, but people always have the freedom to make choices. Regardless of the odds, if you follow the path laid out in the next five chapters, it will take you somewhere good, somewhere whole.

How an affair is disclosed classifies it. If the offending spouse doesn't disclose it, then the offended spouse must discover it, which exacerbates the offense. It works best for the offending spouse to take the initiative and to disclose the affair. You ultimately garner respect for your honesty and courage by doing something honest and courageous.

Honesty with the offended spouse about infidelity represents a turning point in respect to intimacy, and so it is a key step in restoring intimacy. Paradoxically, this revelation represents an act of intimacy with the marital partner. Infidelity is infidelity, but the disclosure of infidelity to the offended spouse falls into the category of fidelity and intimacy.

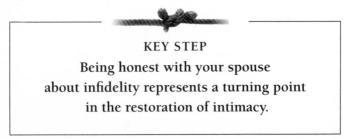

KEY STEP
Being honest with your spouse
about infidelity represents a turning point
in the restoration of intimacy.

In disclosure you begin to return to your original commitment to be honest with your spouse. You begin to present reality with exact accuracy rather than with inaccuracies. In this way honesty begins to re-create intimacy. Recall the secrecy grid introduced in chapter eight.

A = the offending spouse
B = the offended spouse
C = the third party
v = secrets or intimate knowledge or confiding
x = no knowledge of secrets or intimate knowledge or confiding

Disclosure enables the married couple to start recreating this pattern:

A (v), B (v), C (x)

Now the husband and wife share the secrets, the intimate knowledge of the relationship, and in all likelihood no one else knows what they know. The offended spouse moves from an x to a v because secrets and intimate knowledge define the primary or core relationship. At the point of the disclosure everything begins to change.

WHERE TO MAKE THE REVELATION

Experimentation has demonstrated that it's preferable to reveal the infidelity in a counseling session. A therapist can function as a neutral third party, directing the flow to minimize risk factors and maximize the potential for gain. At an unconscious level it says the offending spouse seriously wants to do the right thing in the best way. Disclosure in a counseling setting decreases the volatility and confusion.

Disclosing an affair doesn't normally cause divorce. Phil disclosed to his wife, Megan, that he had an affair. Megan immediately initiated divorce proceedings and would not be deterred. I followed this over time because it did not match the norm. About a year later it became known that she had used Phil's disclosure as a smoke screen while she pursued a simultaneous, undisclosed affair.

People commonly threaten that they would divorce if their spouse has an affair. And sometimes, without the benefit of counseling, perhaps in the event of repeated episodes and minimal efforts at changing by the offending spouse, an offended spouse will initiate a divorce upon disclosure. But generally, disclosing an affair actually functions as part of the marriage healing and transformation process. It's the diagnosis that precedes the treatment.

I usually prepare the offending spouse for the revelation by meeting privately to discuss their secret, either by phone or in person. I then begin the planned disclosure session by asking both parties if either has an agenda for today's session. The offending spouse takes that cue and proceeds.

WHEN TO CONSIDER NOT REVEALING AN AFFAIR

There are times when revealing an affair may be contextually inappropriate. If, for example, you or your spouse is dying, confessing your infidelity may overwhelm other matters that need more attention, such as affirming your love and appreciation for each other regardless of the sins of the past.

If you have experienced domestic violence in your marriage, the revelation of your affair may trigger a recurrence. Some domestic violence specialists believe that any prior domestic violence makes the revelation of an affair unwise. If, however, you wish to reveal an affair and be reconciled with your partner, take the following precautions:

1. Reveal the affair in a highly controlled setting, such as a therapist's office.

2. Establish safety plans with the assistance of family, friends and a domestic violence network, which could involve the use of a safe house.

WHAT IF THE OFFENDING SPOUSE RESISTS DISCLOSING?

"The secret of the extramarital affair is the most important revelation,"[1] one author has said. When initially meeting and evaluating a couple, I let them know that even the most conservative estimates suggest that 11 to 18 percent or more of marital partners have had an affair. I ask them if either of them currently or historically has been in an extramarital affair, and then I say, "If you have been but aren't comfortable disclosing it right now, please call me and let me know privately so we can be thorough in the work we are doing." Perhaps later my phone will ring and the caller will say "You knew I was having an affair, didn't you?" We meet to discuss the situation, and I usually propose proceeding to a disclosure session.

A person's infidelity is sometimes used in divorce proceedings to gain a psychological advantage, but in most states it has no legal weight—a concern that prevents some people from disclosing their affair. Encouraging disclosure and mentioning the frequency with which infidelity occurs can increase the likelihood of a disclosure, which increases the likelihood of healing.

The offended spouse needs to make it safe for the disclosure to take place. You don't create safety by saying, "If you ever cheat on me we're getting a divorce." You create safety with statements like "It would hurt me if you had an affair, but I'd rather know the truth" or "Have you ever had an affair?" or "It may be difficult for you to admit this, but I know you want to be honest, so please trust and respect me by letting me know as soon as possible if you have an affair." Research indicates that self-disclosure encourages further disclosure by others at around the same level. For example, if you say, "I want a totally honest relationship. I can understand that you could have had an affair because I have thought about it myself," you create an environment of safety that makes disclosure more likely for the offending spouse.

DISCOVERY STRATEGIES FOR EXTREME SITUATIONS

Sometimes offending spouses are extremely resistant to disclosure and become very secretive. One well-known website coaches cheating spouses, "When asked about or accused of having an affair—deny, deny, deny." Nevertheless, an affair leaves a trail that can be identified:

- unfamiliar but repeated phone numbers in the "recent calls" list of their cell phone
- unusual websites or e-mail addresses in their computer
- suspicious credit card charges
- unexplained items in their purse, billfold or briefcase
- odd behavior during impromptu phone calls
- unrecognized trips archived on the global position service (GPS) device
- reports from friends of suspicious encounters

Shirley collected stuffed animals. One day her husband, Bob, noticed that she started bringing one to bed and placed it between them. She had never slept with one of her stuffed animals before. She had never had an affair before either. But when her affair started, the stuffed animal came to bed and slept between Shirley and Bob. The covert symbol, the stuffed animal, provided the first clue; shortly thereafter Bob discovered her affair.

The offending spouse often either directly or indirectly discloses their affair. One way or another—by discovery or by disclosure—an affair will inevitably become known. When you know with near certainty that your partner is or has been unfaithful say, "I know you have been involved (had an affair) with someone else." Pause and remain silent. Then say, "Let's talk about it." The disclosure often comes both as a shock and a relief.

What to Reveal

The offending spouse will find it most helpful to be prepared to reveal information simply and factually:

- Who
- What happened (in general terms)
- When

- Where (particularly if on sacred turf)
- Current status (ongoing, terminating or terminated)
- Who else knows

The offending spouse needs to also clarify their commitment to their spouse, marriage and family. This is not a time to color or distort or soft-pedal anything. The simple truth, simply expressed, works best.

Who. The offending spouse should reveal the name of the third party. Failure to do so creates a host of issues. For example, it may seem that the offending spouse has chosen to protect the third party or wishes to keep the door open to continue the affair. Refusing to reveal the name of the third party communicates a lack of trust.

If the offending spouse fears some form of retaliation, they can discuss their reservations about naming the third party and come to mutually acceptable terms prior to the disclosure. The offending spouse might say "I want to reveal the identity of the third party to you but will only do so if you can make a commitment to never initiate contacting them."

What happened in general terms. You should disclose the type of extramarital affair according to the terms detailed in chapter two. Was it a sexual, nonpenetrating or mental affair? Do not disclose details beyond that. More details create mental images which can be hard for the offended spouse to erase. Avoid the sordid details.

When. The offending spouse can reveal when the incident occurred, such as "In late May." The timeline of the affair can be helpful; the offending spouse could say, "The affair occurred between the months of June and August" or "It started last April and has continued."

Where (particularly if at home or on sacred turf). The affair may have occurred out of town on business trips or in town at the third party's apartment. This question becomes particularly important if the affair occurred on the turf of the offended spouse, such as the marital home or bedroom, or the family car. Replacement is appropriate when feasible; it provides a fresh start and eliminates a potentially large and negative trigger for both the offending and offended spouse. Enough negative triggering will occur without overburdening the system.

Sacred turf refers to cherished places such as a favorite restaurant or vacation spot. If the offending spouse went there with the third party, that should also be revealed.

Current status. It only makes sense to disclose whether the affair continues, is terminating or has terminated. Each situation requires a significantly different response because each represents a different level of risk and complexity. The ongoing affair creates the greatest challenge; the affair that has terminated still will create shockwaves but has understandably less risk and complexity. The key steps that we cover later will provide further guidance about these various situations.

Who else knows. Also disclose who else knows about the affair. Keeping the disclosure circle as small as possible is another key step. Too many people knowing about the situation or getting involved may create a huge information management issue. Remember the secrecy grid? The husband and wife should be the primary repository of intimate information. Shared secrets contribute to the rebuilding of their bond and intimacy. Keep the circle only as large as is necessary for healing to occur. The ideal size might be three to five people: the married couple, the therapist, the third party and the partner of the third party if one exists.

Should the disclosure circle include your spiritual counselor? The outcome from this disclosure varies widely and unpredictably. Clergy with special training or experience in this area with good results can add significant value to the process. But in general the bigger disclosure circle adds confusion and unnecessary residual aftereffects to an already confusing situation.

Family and friends tend to offer polarized advice: "Divorce him!" or "You must stay married no matter what!" Rarely do these well-

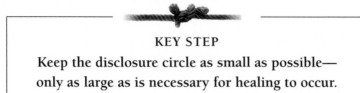

KEY STEP

**Keep the disclosure circle as small as possible—
only as large as is necessary for healing to occur.**

meaning parties offer tools for moving through the process. Couples need a neutral facilitator to empower them to process the affair together.

THE REVELATION SESSION

A good therapist will keep the disclosure of an affair focused on the details that really need to be revealed. From there, the couple needs to work together to address the immediate and systemic problems in their relationship revealed in the affair. You need to look at and talk to each other—experiencing sound communication rather than just learning about it is crucial. A good therapist prompts and facilitates this direct discussion, offering insight into the experience afterward.[2]

The offended spouse may ask, "How could you have done this to me?" This phrase may sound like a question, but it is not and should not be answered. A more appropriate response is simply to hear and summarize what the offended spouse actually means to state: perhaps something as simple as "You're saying to me that you're in shock."

Immediately after her husband disclosed his affair, Ellen said "OK that's it, we're done." Then she bolted out of the room. I followed Ellen to the parking lot, where we talked. She was simply acting out her shock and just needed a few minutes before continuing. Moments later we reconvened and continued.

After the revelation, a good exercise is to think back to a point in time where your relationship was good. Usually your relationship was good early on or you would not have married in the first place. You can then contextualize the affair within your whole history and start to

KEY STEP

**Incorporate reliable, professional experience
throughout the process of overcoming infidelity.**

consider a few very simple goals. The questions might go like this:

- What originally attracted us to each other?
- Have we ever had really good times in our marriage?
- It used to be better, now it's worse; what should our goals be?

The most simple basic goals are to get through this crisis, stay to-gether, and make a solid marriage and future.

Perhaps you notice a subtle allusion to traditional marriage vows: to have and to hold, for better, for worse. If a couple ever experienced attraction for one another and chooses to implement state-of-the-art relationship training, they can have an outstanding outcome: a happy ending. Hope is critical at this stage; if your therapist isn't helping you reestablish hope in your relationship, you should seek out another counselor.

Gradually your focus should shift from the affair to its cause and meaning for your marriage. Like an autopsy, knowing the cause does not alter the past, but knowing somehow gives us some closure about the past and our immediate pain. Knowing also equips us to make more intelligent future decisions.

This often is deferred to a later session. In the first session I concentrate on the disclosure, what needs to be revealed, and learning how to share more effectively—big-picture issues.[3]

Both spouses should clarify their commitment to one another, the marriage and the family. Sometimes so much confusion exists about direction that one or both parties choose not to make this assertion. But if either party can, it helps a great deal.

THE ESSENTIAL DISCIPLINE FOR COMMUNICATION: SHARE

The goal of sharing is to understand and be understood. That goal is reached as people take turns as presenter and empowerer. Presenters are storytellers, sharing their perspective or viewpoint regarding some issue or subject. By contrast, empowerers are active listeners, concentrating on the perspective of the other person—summarizing and harmonizing with the presenter. Empowerers extend themselves toward the presenter, acknowledging their feelings and retelling key elements of the story.

Wisdom suggests that the lower-motivated person needs to spend more time in the role of the presenter. Think about it for a moment. The higher-motivated person does not need as much attention—they are already motivated. Rather, the lower-motivated person needs to be empowered to become more motivated.

The price a home sells for provides an example of this. If the seller has a low level of motivation to sell, the price of the home will remain high. By contrast, if the homebuyer has a low level of motivation to buy, the price will become lower. A natural shift in pricing occurs in the favor of the lowest-motivated person. The SHARE process, by empowering and extending, engenders motivation.

Typically in the revelation phase, the offending spouse first presents, using the guidelines articulated earlier in this chapter. The offended spouse empowers primarily by summarizing what they heard. This important stage should not be skipped because it immediately creates an active dialogue, slows things down and confirms the accuracy of what the presenter expressed and what the empower heard.

In the emotional intensity of a disclosure, however, the roles will switch rapidly. The offended spouse needs to be empowered to present their feelings. Ultimately there are five phases of the SHARE process, but especially early on, couples may linger in the first three phases, with the offended spouse in the role of presenter and the offending spouse spending a lot of time harmonizing and acknowledging the feelings of the offended partner. The empowerer works to . . .

1. Summarize
   - "Is there anything you want to say?"
   - "You said . . ."
2. Harmonize
   - "Help me understand your viewpoint." or
   - "I see your point of view because . . ."
3. Acknowledge feelings
   - "How do or did you feel?"
   - "You feel or felt . . ."
   - "Can you recall the first or most important time you felt like this?"
   - "Can you recall a distant time you felt like this not related to me?"
4. Recycle
   - Continue to summarize, harmonize and acknowledge feelings as needed.
   - Move on to extend yourself to your partner when you're confident that the presenter has been fully heard and understood.
5. Extend
   - "Is there more?"
   - "Is it enough that I understand or could I help in some way?"
   - "What new, positive trait would you like me to focus on?"
   - "What specifically could I do or say that would help?"
   - "I can commit to that."
   - "For now, here is what I can commit to . . ."

About half the time, once someone has met with me and prepared to disclose their infidelity, it comes out in between sessions. Generally the preparation helps things go fairly well. Sam and Samantha had been married ten years and parented two young children. Sam called me after a session and confided that he had been secretly involved in a three-month affair with a recently divorced woman from his athletic club. He wanted to meet to discuss what to do. When we met, Sam confirmed his desire to stay married. "I used to love Samantha, I'm very close to our kids, and I want to end the affair. In fact, I've been trying to end it now for two months, but we keep getting back together." We discussed how revealing the affair could greatly help Sam achieve his desire to finally end it with the third party. We concluded with a plan to disclose the affair at the next scheduled session.

Sam and Samantha arrived at the next session looking somewhat preoccupied. Samantha almost immediately spoke up, began to tear a little and said Sam had told her the night before about his affair. "It's been a long night and a tough day. What I can't understand is how Sam could do what he did. I would not dream of hurting Sam that way." Sam added, "It just came up so I decided to go ahead and tell Samantha."

Since the disclosure already occurred I suggested we talk about the cause of the affair. Samantha said "I really have no idea. I still can't believe this has occurred." Sam answered that it was not really about some cause; the affair occurred just because the third party was there. I proceeded to review and ask questions about what generally contributes to affairs; Sam resonated with the concept of landmarks and competency. Having been married for ten years, he felt somewhat bored, as though everything seemed the same. His work had also become stagnant. He felt like he could go no further in his job for the foreseeable future. The affair in part created excitement and gave Sam a sense of power and competency. The affair also, of course, created confusion, guilt, anxiety and preoccupation.

Then Samantha said to Sam, "Why couldn't you have talked to me about what you were feeling instead of having an affair?" At first Sam started to answer Samantha's question, but I interrupted: Samantha's question was really a statement. We shifted into the SHARE method; Sam took the role of empowerer. "Samantha, you're saying I should have talked to you, my wife, about what I was feeling and thinking." With a mixture of tears and anger Samantha replied, "Right!"

Next I invited Sam to harmonize: "Can you let her know you understand or at least recognize where she's coming from? Can you validate her viewpoint?" Sam spoke in a disarmingly sincere tone: "Samantha, you are absolutely right. If I was feeling this disconnected from you or disheartened at work, I should have been talking about it with you—not letting it build up till I did something stupid and destructive." Samantha acknowledged that she felt understood by Sam, so I invited Sam to guess what Samantha was feeling. Sam said to his wife "You probably feel hurt and angry." Samantha clarified: "I feel devastated and anxious. I'm devastated that one of the persons I most trusted and loved disappointed me, and now I'm anxious if it has really ended or could happen again."

Sam, catching on to the SHARE process, resisted the temptation to defend himself or to reassure Samantha. Instead he recycled, summarizing, harmonizing and acknowledging her feelings again based on what she had just added. "Samantha, I can tell that you are devastated and disappointed. And I can understand why too, because in the past we used to be able to talk through tough issues. So I can see why you might be anxious about the affair continuing or about this happening again in the future."

Sam then extended himself to Samantha. "Is there anything else you want to say at this time?" When she said, "Not now," Sam went on: "Is it enough that I understand, or could I help in some way?" Samantha replied, "It's enough now that you just understand. Thanks."

The biggest and most important task for the offending spouse is to *listen without defending*. The biggest and most important task for the offended spouse is to *speak without offending*. Samantha felt Sam empowering her by using this process. Though her pain did not stop, it lessened a little, and she had a glint of hope. At the same

- *Live without pretending,*
- *Love without depending,*
- *Listen without defending,*
- *Speak without offending,*
- *Give without ending,*
- *Build without rending.*

NINA ROBERTA BAKER

time Sam began to go through a huge metamorphosis. He learned that he could listen without defending. He learned that empowering ultimately yields good results.

Regardless of whether you fall into the role of the offending spouse or the offended spouse, it works best to take responsibility and confess your part of the problem, while seeking to understand one another. The SHARE process helps this occur. The empowerer systematically seeks to understand the presenter. And as you trade roles, both parties feel heard and can more likely address and fulfill their yearnings.

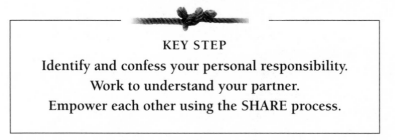

KEY STEP
Identify and confess your personal responsibility.
Work to understand your partner.
Empower each other using the SHARE process.

"But the affair is his/her fault," you might protest. Over the years I've come to the conclusion that when all the factors get laid on the table, the fault approximates these percentages:

- 25 percent his fault
- 25 percent her fault

- 25 percent their fault (i.e., how the couple interacts)
- 25 percent other factors' fault (e.g., other people, finances, work)

These percentages somewhat accurately depict the role each party plays in pressurizing the relationship and increasing the risk of an affair. Certainly the full blame for acting out an affair falls on the offending spouse, But both the offended and the offending spouse cope and heal more rapidly when each takes responsibility for the evolution of affair conditions.

Wherever you think the percentages fall, be quick to engage in a fearless and searching personal inventory of your part of the problem, take responsibility for that and confess it. Vigorously dedicate yourself to understanding your partner. You cannot throw garbage on another without also soiling yourself. Blame and criticism have a deleterious effect upon your partner and more dangerously upon yourself.

ONCE AND FOR ALL

The revelation works best with full, though controlled, disclosure. If you have had multiple affairs, the best time for revealing them occurs during the initial disclosure. The offended spouse will go through somewhat predictable stages of recovery. If you reveal a partial list of the past affairs and more comes out later, the offended spouse will likely experience a loss of confidence in you and extended suffering. You lose credibility at a critical point when you need all the help you can get building credibility back up again.

Infidelity could be likened to a traumatic injury. The primary injury needs some time to heal before one can begin a course of rehabilitation. Infidelity issues fade over time but slowly at first. Typically it requires one to three months from the point of disclosure for the dust to settle enough to begin substantive work on the marriage proper.

SUMMARY

It may be exhilarating to climb a high peak. But the thin air, deprived of oxygen, makes you feel like you're suffocating, and your body's organs start shutting down. At the peak, lightning strikes occur frequently. Hypothermia poses a constant threat. If you stay there long it will kill you. You must descend in order to live and to be restored to wholeness.

When it comes to infidelity, descent usually necessitates disclosure. The revelation of an affair most safely occurs in the office of an experienced therapist. The therapist or offended spouse can play a key role in decreasing resistance and increasing the likelihood of disclosure, but the offending spouse usually reveals the affair in some direct or indirect manner and the offended spouse usually knows this at some level.

The goal at this point is to reestablish honest and open communication. The offending spouse should only disclose the necessary details of the affair to the offended spouse. The SHARE method guides the communication process, empowering both partners.

It is one thing to get up a mountain; it is another thing to get down a mountain. The disclosure or discovery of infidelity often generates high level trauma—perhaps second only to the death of a child. The next chapter examines how to handle this trauma.

—10—

The Crisis

Reconciling with Your Spouse

Focus: Conflict Resolution
Goal: Transform the Negative.
Process: Explore the Problem and Generate Solutions
Key Essential Discipline: RECONCILE

Andy Politz has summited the highest peak in the world, Mount Everest, multiple times. On one occasion he helped rescue a party of five—a friend, the friend's client from Guatemala and three Russian climbers. They had spent the night near the peak in bad conditions. Another party had come across them but left the party for dead, giving them only a candy bar to assuage their own guilt. Andy and his party, by contrast, abandoned their climb to devote all their resources to the rescue.

The party in trouble needed oxygen and water, of course, but mostly they needed someone to walk them down the mountain step by step. Every two steps those being rescued would collapse. Generally competent, experienced and strong, now they were temporarily dazed, confused, weak and blind. They could not rescue themselves. They needed somebody to help.

Rescue by definition usually requires others. In most cases you cannot do it alone. In recovering from the crisis that often follows the disclosure or discovery of infidelity, the offended spouse needs to do all they can to help themselves. That often involves having someone walk with them through the trauma.

THE SAGA OF SKIP AND BRENDA

Brenda found hints that Skip might be having an affair. She confronted him about it, and he confirmed her suspicions. A few weeks later Brenda continued to struggle. "I feel miserable," she said. "I'm not suicidal, but sometimes I wish something would just happen to me, like a fatal car crash, to get me out of this mental pain. I obsess on what happened and cry whenever I'm alone. Skip is really trying, and that is meaningful—but it doesn't seem to help how I feel. When Skip confessed, he got rid of the guilt of secrecy and started feeling much better. Since the disclosure I've been in crisis."

Skip began to descend the mountain with his disclosure. Brenda by contrast found herself thrust into high altitude with no acclimatization. She gasped for air but could not recover.

The offended spouse often experiences a crisis after being told of or after discovering the infidelity. This may occur even if an affair was suspected. The offended spouse can expect to go through some predictable stages:

- disorganization
- reorganization
- organization

Disorganization. When you first hear that your spouse has had an affair, you may experience the basic negative emotions of sadness, anger or fear. You may ricochet between them, first feeling angry and then moving quickly to feeling sad. Your thoughts may become disorganized. Sometimes you may even find it difficult to work or address domestic tasks. You might find yourself saying, "I'm worthless at work. I can't get the affair out of my mind."

Many people experience sleep disturbance; they can't sleep very well or they sleep all the time. Some people lose their appetite or feel nauseated when eating and may lose a significant amount of weight. Others increase appetite and put on weight. The immune system may suffer, making you more vulnerable to illness or disease.

Efficient people may become inefficient. Social people may go into hiding. Passive people may act more aggressive. Whatever your normal behavior may be, some changes usually occur.

Amy worked as an OB-GYN. Doug worked as a pilot. Shortly after we met jointly, Doug called to tell me that he had been having an affair for several months with a flight attendant. Amy, a calm and level-headed physician, sat in my office as Doug disclosed. She became visibly agitated, cursed and left the office saying she never wanted to see her husband again. Later she returned to the session as we began to unravel the genesis of Doug's affair and make plans for the immediate situation. In the days to follow, Amy had trouble sleeping and eating. Three days later I got a call from her; she had hospitalized herself due to dehydration. A physician who absolutely knew how to care for the human body experienced disorganization to the point that she required hospitalization.

Reorganization. As you begin to stabilize after learning of the affair, you begin to experience reorganization. An experience, a memory, even the children offer a foothold. You may think, *I couldn't bear the way a separation would hurt the children.* This idea becomes the first plank in rebuilding the future.

Some people experience reorganization as they focus on their core beliefs, values or commitments. If you view your marriage vows as a sacrament or a solemn vow, that may provide the first anchor. "When I said for better or worse I meant it. This is about the worst. But one thing I know for sure is that I will keep my promise to God and to myself."

Here are some other examples of things people say indicating reorganization:

- "We used to have a loving relationship, and I believe we can have that again."

- "Last night when we talked about this you cried, and I know you are sorry for what you have done. That meant a lot to me."
- "You're still wearing your wedding ring."
- "My dog just loves me and never changes; I can hold on to that for now."
- "I feel good when you hold me for about five minutes at least."
- "I'm at least OK at work now. It lets me get my mind off us for a while."

When reorganization occurs you feel it. Gradually these planks or anchors begin to accumulate and outweigh the sense of disorganization.

Organization. Finally the pieces come together. The structure of life may be significantly different, but it works.

Scott and Elaine sold their house, moved to a different neighborhood and created a new core group of friends. Their old friends drank a lot of alcohol and played the social scene. Their new friends drank more modestly and often discussed their spiritual values.

Same suburb, new home, new friends . . . this provides just one example. Organization may take many different forms.

POST-TRAUMATIC STRESS

Infidelity issues fade over time but slowly at first. The disclosure often creates a crisis that hits with traumatic intensity. Many people steadily move through the stages of disorganization, reorganization and organization. But some people seem to get stuck.

If you receive quality professional care and you still feel overwhelmed and obsessively preoccupied with the infidelity after one to three months, you may be experiencing something somewhat like post-traumatic stress disorder (PTSD). You may want to discuss treatment options with your therapist.[1]

Ted and Barb had been married for ten years. One day Ted asked his daughter to get a gift he had for her in his briefcase. Barb helped her daughter look, and in the process found an explicit love letter addressed to Ted. When she confronted him, he disclosed a five-year ongoing affair. The affair had gone on for half their marriage.

Barb, normally a capable and optimistic person, found herself chronically depressed and obsessed with Ted's affair. She kept imagining Ted and the third party making love. Even though Ted did everything he could to help Barb recover—even when we considered that Ted had spent only two hundred hours with the third party, as opposed to the twenty thousand hours he had spent with Barb over the same period—nothing seemed to help. Barb was stuck.

I suggested we meet individually to specifically help her move past the trauma. We did a session of therapy tailored toward PTSD;[2] at the next session Barb announced that she'd made up her mind to get past the old images. The last week had been better for her than the past two months. Often it requires only one or two sessions of this nature for the offended spouse to gain ground. Like getting over a hill, sometimes we need only a little extra power or assistance.

SHOULD WE CONTINUE TO LIVE TOGETHER?

Unless there's real potential for physical abuse, continue to live together as you process the crisis. No matter how "poor" your initial reasons—for the kids, to save money, to avoid legal difficulties or extended family disputes, out of convenience or habit—in time, as you do appropriate work, you will likely discover excellent reasons to stay married.

Staying together saves money and time and minimizes the disruption to everyday life for the children and for the couple. You are less likely to wonder what each other is doing because you are more likely to know. Beyond that, however, it matches the reality of the marriage document: things were better, and now they're worse, but you are staying together. Living together also makes it much easier to do the work indicated for this stage.

Take good care of yourself physically during this time of crisis. Eat, exercise and sleep regularly. Get your physician to test you for sexually transmitted disease and prescribe appropriate medication if necessary for your physical or mental health.

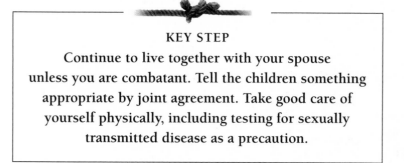

KEY STEP
Continue to live together with your spouse
unless you are combatant. Tell the children something
appropriate by joint agreement. Take good care of
yourself physically, including testing for sexually
transmitted disease as a precaution.

Tell the children something appropriate, preferably by joint agreement. You might say to them, "You may have noticed me crying or acting upset. That's because your mother/father and I are working on a problem." Perhaps your children may ask "What kind of problem?" You could answer, "It's an adult (relationship) problem. I'm not going to get into the details. You have problems sometimes too, don't you— problems that make you sad or mad?" Mostly children have a more concrete orientation versus an abstract one. They want to know what, if anything, will change for them. If nothing much will change, that's about all they want and need to know for now.

Sometimes I'm asked if the children should be told that their father or mother had an affair. I do think it best serves the long-term interest of the children to know that an affair occurred. However, the appropriate timing of this disclosure may surprise you. My bias is to tell your children about the affair only after they have married as adults. Now facing some of the same forces that led to infidelity in your marriage, your disclosure may serve to inoculate your children against the same patterns. Adult children are also more capable of putting the disclosure into a meaningful and beneficial context.

THE MESSAGE YOU NEED TO GET

The offending spouse often initiates or participates in an affair in part because of an underlying conscious or unconscious unmet need. The unmet need is the message you need to get. You do not need to get or possess the messenger.

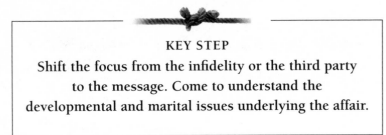

KEY STEP

Shift the focus from the infidelity or the third party to the message. Come to understand the developmental and marital issues underlying the affair.

Daniel, born a twin, had a father who worked as a traveling salesman and a mother who remained self-absorbed and detached. Lacking clear guidance and nurture, the twins had a fierce sibling rivalry. Eventually Daniel got married seeking attachment and connection. At first, marriage seemed to meet his need for connection and attachment, but as inevitable conflicts came into the picture, Daniel sought connection and attachment through an affair. He became enamored with the messenger (the third party) and married her. He did not yet get the message. This cycle repeated itself through three marriages—and three marriage-ending affairs. As an old man whose financial status had been ravaged by three divorces, Daniel finally had a breakthrough: his profound need for connection was met through his newly found personal faith. He finally got the message.

Had Daniel's wives made the shift from messenger to message, perhaps one of them could have forgiven Daniel for his infidelity and welcomed reconciliation. When the offended spouse obsesses about the atrocity of the affair, he or she will likely fail to see what it means. Both partners need to understand the developmental and marital issues or needs underlying the affair. Daniel simply needed attachment and connection. Both Daniel and his wives failed to get the message and understand the meaning of his affairs.

Once husband and wife understand the message, next they need to convert the message into meaningful application in the marriage. Daniel needed attachment and connection. He could have requested that his wife be more available and responsive to him. He could have further detailed this by suggesting what she could do to be seen by him as available and responsive. Perhaps Daniel could have suggested:

- "Be available to me, if you can, by simply saying, 'I'm committed to you and to our family. I pledge to talk to you promptly about any issue you have.' "

- "Be responsive to me, if you can, by making love to me once or twice most weeks."

Daniel's wife could shift her thinking from *Daniel rejected me by having an affair* to *Daniel actually was seeking attachment and connection through my availability and response.*

KEY STEP
**Begin to apply the message to the marriage
and be patient.**

As husband and wife successfully decode and apply the message underneath the affair, healing starts to occur. It takes patience because healing takes time. In the latter portion of this chapter, this process will be detailed more fully.

DEALING WITH DIFFERENT NEEDS

Both husband and wife have strong and perhaps divergent needs at this point. The offending spouse may need to discover and address their core inner need—perhaps for connection. The offended spouse may not yet be prepared to connect. Thousands of different variations of competing needs exist because people are unique.

So what should be done with these needs or competing needs? Ask for anything. Request anything from your partner that could address your need. Ask in positive and specific ways.

- "Could you call me if you leave the office and make sure I can reach you by cell phone?"
- "Could you change your cell phone number and only give it to people I approve?"
- "Could you just hold me for five minutes?"
- "Could we talk about our heavy issues for only thirty minutes a night, after the kids go to bed, so I don't get flooded and overwhelmed?"

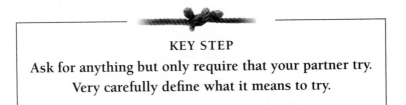

KEY STEP
Ask for anything but only require that your partner try. Very carefully define what it means to try.

If your partner can't give you what you request, ask them to propose their closest alternative. You ask, "Can we start sleeping in the same bed again?" Your partner replies "You can bring the rollaway in for a trial next weekend; I'm comfortable with that for now." When your partner gives you what you request or proposes their closest alternative, it shows they are trying. Very carefully and reasonably keep defining what it means to try. A seasoned therapist can greatly help at this point by clarifying reasonable requests and by providing creative alternatives.

If your partner is not trying at all, in many cases they have already functionally initiated a divorce. Whether you want a divorce or dissolution or not, every state has a means for a divorce to be forced by the hand of the party who wants it. As an alternative, consider meeting with a mediator. A mediator explains the laws of your state that apply to divorce or dissolution and helps each party assess what they most value regarding assets, child visitation and so on. It's a process of discovery that involves disclosing and proving your actual assets. The mediator then begins to draft a document suitable for use in a legal dissolution or divorce. Along the way the mediator will guide you into finding agreement as disputes come up.

Mediation has several advantages that can actually serve to mend the marriage:

- Mediation keeps both parties talking and learning to make agreements. Sometimes this ability creates hope for the marriage.

- Mediation lets both parties face the harsh realities of asset distribution and child visitation schedules. Sometimes as people count the cost they reconsider their path and begin trying to mend.[3]

- Mediation provides a form of tough love and reverse psychology. If you clearly say to your partner that you want to mend the marriage while also progressing through mediation, you are less likely to be identified as the problem. If you resist mediation it usually sets up a power struggle that showcases the worst traits of each party.

- Even if mediation does not result in a decision to save the marriage, husband and wife will more quickly establish relationships of mutual respect and perhaps friendship. In most cases this has long-term value for both parties, whether married or not.

- Generally this process saves considerable money over contested divorce or dissolution proceedings involving considerable expense for combatant lawyers. You mostly pay for the services of one mediator instead of two arguing lawyers.

Mediation is not a legal proceeding. Along the way or when you finish, most mediators will advise you to have your attorney look over the completed document. The mediator can incorporate recommendations from your attorney into the document at your request.

It may take a few months to go through mediation. Lots can change in a few months. In some cases marriages experience mending, and ultimately reconciliation, when a partner who refuses to try will agree to counseling and mediation. Some couples go through counseling and mediation, dissolve their marriage, remarry each other and move on to achieve the marriage of their dreams. Those who fight their way through divorce and dissolution for whatever reason have less hopeful probabilities or possibilities.

In order to survive a marital crisis like infidelity, however, a couple needs to reconcile. The next section will outline how to reconcile effectively.

The Essential Discipline for Conflict Resolution: RECONCILE

The goal of reconciling is to transform the negative. We reach that goal by exploring the problem and generating solutions.

The process of reconciliation may look overwhelming and complex at first. Like a recipe, which involves assembling several ingredients, combining them in a certain manner, then cooking and serving accordingly, after a while the reconciliation process becomes natural and perhaps automatic. Once you've mastered the essentials of the formula, you can get creative.

Figure 10.1 simplistically presents how our minds typically function. Figure 10.2 has been filled out to demonstrate how the mind functions when negatively triggered. The left side captures the natural, reactive, negative, or what I call the broken response. By contrast the right side captures the supernatural, proactive, positive or what I call the whole choice. The goal is to get from the left side to the right side.

Broken Present	Whole Present
1. The triggering comment, behavior, or situation is . . .	11. Verify the trigger as true: • Assume the trigger will occur again. • The triggering comment, behavior, or situation is . . .
2. My negative spontaneous thoughts: (I think that . . .)	12. Give the benefit of the doubt (My positive and life-giving thoughts are . . .)
Negative Responses **3.** I emotionally feel . . . 4. I physically feel . . . 5. I act this out by . . .	Positive Responses 13. I emotionally feel . . . 14. I physically feel . . . 15. I act this out by . . .
Broken Past	**Whole Past**
6. This brings back bad memories of . . .	16. Appreciate and celebrate the past (This brings back good memories of . . .) • Achievements • Successes • Victories • Models • Examples
7. This brings back bad childhood memories of . . .	17. This brings back good childhood memories of . . .
Broken Future	**Whole Future**
8. I perceive the other person, myself or the situation as having the negative trait(s) . . .	18. Be (I desire the other person, myself or the situation to have the following positive trait[s]):
9. I vowed (at the time of the incident) to get back at them, myself, or it in the future by . . .	19. Do (I propose the following positive, measurable and specific future suggestions/commitments): a.
10. I vowed (at the time of the incident) to protect myself in future by . . .	b. c.

Figure 10.1. The mental process of reconciliation. Generally only the bold numbered items in the left column are safe to express, whereas anything in the right column can be expressed.

Broken Present

1. The triggering comment, behavior or situation is . . .
E: Is there anything you want to say?
P: It's tearing me apart that you had an affair with Charlotte.
E: (Summarize) Hearing about my affair really tears at you.

2. My negative spontaneous thoughts are . . .
P: I can't believe it. You are so selfish. You are a jerk. All you must care about is sex. You have ruined our family. I'll never be able to feel the same about you again. I can't trust you.
E: (Harmonize) I can understand your viewpoint because it is hard to believe. It was selfish of me. And I know it looks like all I cared about was sex. What I did has really messed things up. I can see how it would be hard to trust me right now.

3. My negative emotional responses are . . .
E: How do you feel?
P: I feel both angry and sad.
E: (Acknowledge feelings) You feel angry and sad.

4. My negative physical responses are . . .
P: I feel sick, like I'm going to throw up, and my heart is pounding like crazy.

5. I act this out by . . .
P: I'm shaking, and I can't stop crying. First I can't stand to be in the same room with you and want to be alone. Then I want you to hold me and say you're sorry.
E: (Acknowledge feelings) I know how angry and sad you are. It's confusing—you feel this then you feel that. And it's hitting you physically and affecting what you do.

Broken Past

6. This brings back bad memories of . . .
E: Out of curiosity, can you recall the first or most important time you felt like this?
P: Somewhat this reminds me of the time our daughter had surgery and you did not leave work to spend the day with me.
E: (Summarize) This reminds you of me not being there the day our daughter had surgery.
E: (Harmonize) Frankly I don't remember the situation the same way, but I can understand that if you wanted me there or needed me there and I wasn't, that would disappoint you.

7. This brings back bad childhood memories of . . .
E: Can you recall the first or most important time you felt like this—not related to me?
P: It was overwhelming when dad was in the car accident and we did not know if he would live through the night.
E: (Acknowledge feelings) This makes you feel overwhelmed like you felt as a child when your dad had the accident.

Broken Future

8. I perceive the other person, myself or the situation as having the negative trait of being . . .
P: You are selfish. You are a jerk. You are untrustworthy. I am weak. I am unappealing.

9. I vowed (at the time of the incident) to get back at them, myself or it in the future by . . .
P: I hope some day you suffer the way I am right now.

10. I vowed (at the time of the incident) to protect myself in future by . . .
P: I'll never again let myself love you or trust you like I did.

Figure 10.2. An example of the mental process of reconciliation

Whole Present

11. *Verify the trigger as true by checking for accuracy. Did I accurately hear or see what I thought I heard or saw?*
P: Yes, my husband said he had an affair with Charlotte.

12. *Give the benefit of the doubt: My positive and life giving thoughts are . . .*
E: May I ask what you would be thinking if you were to give me (yourself/others/the situation) the benefit of the doubt?
P: I married you because you thought of others. And I know you care about more things than sex. In time I believe and hope that I will be able to love you and trust you again.
E: (Harmonize) I agree. I do think about and care about others including you. And sex is secondary in my life compared to the importance of family and many other things. And I'm excited to hear that you think I can regain your trust because even though I broke our trust I truly want to be fully trustworthy both now and in the future.

13. *I emotionally feel . . .*
E: How do you feel now?
P: I still feel sad but not as angry. OK for now.
E: (Acknowledge Feelings) You feel sad but less angry and OK.
P: Right.

14. *I physically feel . . .*
E: Physically I'm a little more calm and settled.

15. *I act this out by . . .*
P: I'm more comfortable being in the same room with you. I just want to know more about what caused this to happen.
E: (Summarize) You want to know more about the cause. Me too. That would be good.

Whole Past

16. *Appreciate and celebrate the past: achievements, successes, models and examples. This brings back good memories of . . .*
E: This brings back good memories of . . .
P: We have both faced major challenges before and have worked our way through it like when you could not get that job you wanted.
E: (Harmonize) Yes we have had some hits and worked our way through them such as the AJA deal.

17. *This brings back good childhood memories of . . .*
E: This brings back good childhood memories of . . .
P: I recall how wonderful I felt when we knew dad would live after the accident and likely be OK again.
E: (Acknowledge feeling) You felt wonderful when your dad got better. Now you feel at least a little bit wonderful.

Whole Future

18. *Encourage and inspire traits: I desire the other person, myself or the situation to have the positive trait of being . . .*
E: What new, positive trait would you desire (yourself/others) to focus on? What do you want me to be?
P: I know you want to be sensitive, protective and trustworthy. I want to be strong and I know I am attractive. Perhaps I can work on it too.

19. *Suggestions/Commitments: My positive, measurable and specific future suggestions/ commitments to others, myself or for the situation are . . .*
E: What positive, measurable and specific actions could I (you/others) take or words could I (you/others) say that would help? (In this particular situation what could I do or say to help you see me as being sensitive, protective and trustworthy?)
P: Please write a letter to Charlotte ending the relationship. Let me read it and make sure I'm comfortable with what you say. Then send it by Tuesday. Go out of your way to reassure me about your schedule at this time.
E: OK, I can commit to that.

In this example the offended spouse is the presenter (P) and the offending spouse is the empowerer (E). The first, third and seventh statements are the most beneficial to the presenter on the broken side; they get to the heart of the matter and the underlying issues that the current conflict has triggered. At different points the presenter and empowerer roles would understandably switch—both parties need to be heard and empowered, both parties need to move from brokenness to wholeness. You will recognize the empower using the SHARE communication tools: summarize, harmonize, acknowledge feelings, recycle and extend.

Always determine presenter and empowerer roles, and stay in your role until the entire process reaches completion. Trade roles then and only then. If either party breaks role for a moment, get back into the proper role as soon as possible. A counselor can direct traffic. Just being clear about the presenter and the empowerer roles helps a lot. Later on when couples have gotten used to the exercise, I encourage them to work through the steps on paper when they experience conflict, then use what they've written to present. Doing so enables you to explore the problem and generate solutions.

In this section the presenter may choose to look at the situation from a supernatural, proactive, positive and whole perspective. Often the presenter needs help in doing this. They frequently can't get there on their own very easily. This book helps. A skilled counselor helps. And ultimately the empowerer helps. If the presenter can't come up with an idea that works for them (which is common), we simply offer some suggestions.

Regardless of the disagreements or issues, people can usually reach consensus when they focus on positive traits (statement 18) and suggestions (statement 19). When a couple moves through these steps as directed, with one in the presenter role and the other in the empowerer role, they effectively explore the problem and generate solutions. Mastering the reconcilitation process is an essential discipline. Most good conflict resolution methods, when evaluated, embody the elements found in the reconciliation process.

On the whole side of the reconciliation process, anything can be expressed. The key involves converting broken, negative spontaneous thoughts into whole, positive and life-giving thoughts which give the benefit of the doubt. Convert statement 2, for example, into statement 12. Below are several classic examples of broken versus whole thinking:

Broken: This affair is all his/her fault.
Whole: Responsibility for the affair is divided among both spouses, the structure of the relationship and external factors.

Broken: My partner is sick to have a relationship or sex with someone else.
Whole: Since we are all profoundly social and sexual in nature, this was a natural and logical (though tragic) thing to occur.

Broken: No one can ever really get over this.
Whole: Over time, as we approach this with wisdom, it will become a distant memory from which we profited.

Broken: My partner had sex with another person.
Whole: If we can figure out what pushed or pulled my partner into an affair, our own relationship may become more intimate.

Broken: The worst thing is the dishonesty.
Whole: My partner is right now being honest with me about one of the hardest things to reveal.

Broken: How could my partner carry on an affair for so long?
Whole: My partner chose to reconnect with me even after such a long period of infidelity.

Broken: Once a cheater, always a cheater.

Whole: What we are learning and becoming through this process makes a repeat unlikely.

Broken: If I forgive my partner, they will be more likely to do it again.
Whole: Both of us are suffering in different ways. If I do not eventually forgive my partner, it will ultimately hurt me and increase the risk of a repeat.

Broken: You will never change. I can't believe in you.
Whole: I know this time is very tumultuous and confusing, but I believe you are in the process of making necessary corrections and wise choices. I believe in you.

Broken: I want to kill you or myself. I want to leave you forever.
Whole: I made a promise to stick with you for better or worse. I intend to keep my word.

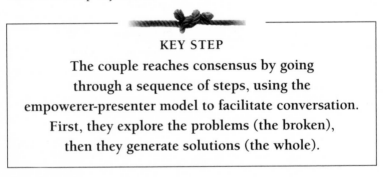

KEY STEP
The couple reaches consensus by going
through a sequence of steps, using the
empowerer-presenter model to facilitate conversation.
First, they explore the problems (the broken),
then they generate solutions (the whole).

A SERIOUS CAUTION

The intentional disclosure or coincidental discovery of infidelity often creates a crisis. The crisis must be managed effectively or the results may prove life threatening. Many counselors who specialize in treating infidelity confirm that suicidal thoughts often accompany a disclosure to the offended spouse. As one author put it, "What you want to kill is not yourself but your pain."[4] Older men have a particularly high risk of suicide, perhaps due to higher rates of depression, physical strength and knowledge of lethal means.

Bill, about sixty years old, woke up one day to a note from his wife saying she had left him for peace of mind and for another man. Bill promised to stop drinking alcohol and be nicer. Over the next few weeks he contacted Shirley repeatedly, but she steadfastly confirmed her decision. Bill drank himself to sleep, cried, languished about his misery with one friend. He went to see his physician at the veterans' hospital and talked about the situation. The doctor, concerned for Bill's well-being, asked him to reschedule for next week. Bill left without rescheduling, went home, had his last drink and committed suicide with his gun.

Natalie, a nurse in her thirties, discovered her husband embroiled in an affair with a coworker at the university where he taught. Micah and Natalie argued and screamed at each other. Micah would not stop seeing the third party. The next day at work Natalie went into the drug closet, filled a syringe and injected herself with a lethal dose in the thigh. She walked out of the closet, got a drink of water at the fountain and collapsed. The next day she awakened. Available emergency assistance saved her. She sought professional counseling assistance. Today she cannot believe she threatened her own life. She has remarried, heads the nursing staff and enjoys life.

Oddly enough, the descent into wholeness involves temporarily putting your partner into a crisis state. The offending spouse has been in the death zone for a while, so descending lets them breathe a little easier. By contrast, the offended spouse feels like they have been dropped into the death zone of a mountain peak without any acclimatization. The necessary disclosure hits the offended spouse hard.

The offended spouse experiences this crisis in many systems: their senses, thoughts, emotions, physiology and behavior all get involved. This needs to happen. They are in the right place, but they feel miserable.

The reconciliation process enables the couple to explore the problem and generate solutions. As the immediate crisis following the disclosure or discovery of the affair settles down, major decisions yet need to be made. Future paths must be determined. You do not want to spend long at higher elevations. Getting off the mountain and back on level ground becomes a matter of urgency.

—11—

Realignment

Redefining Your Character

Focus: Character Development and Commitment
Goal: Be Your Best.
Process: Be Defined by Positive Character Traits
Key Essential Discipline: REFINE

After the disclosure and its resultant crisis comes realignment. Realignment involves the critical decision about your future path and your companion. Will you align yourself with your spouse or take another path?

If you experienced only sexual or only emotional infidelity, the decision to realign with your spouse might be easy. If, however, the infidelity involved both sex and a relationship of some significance, you might find the realignment process agonizingly complex, and you may be mired down in indecision.

This chapter brings order to these different scenarios. As climbers descend the mountain peak they face similar quandaries. Which path shall we take? Shall we retrace the path we took to get to this destination? Should we take a different path altogether? Do we need to abandon our gear? Do we face survival issues? How much time do we have to decide? One thing remains certain: the path you choose will create your destiny. You will be seen as wise or foolish, daring or conservative.

Whether the descent involves taking a different route or the same route, virtually all climbers say the descent feels harder. During ascent, summit fever drives climbers. During descent, motivation wanes, reserves may be depleted, and you ache more.

Your philosophy may influence the path you choose. If you have a philosophy of sacrifice and ultimate right and wrong (honor), then you may choose a path of marital reconciliation. If you have a philosophy of freedom to pursue what you feel (expediency), then you may choose a path in pursuit of the third party.[1] If you remain unclear or confused about your philosophy, this stage may drive you crazy as you vacillate, first making one decision, then changing your mind, only to reverse again and again.

We will examine four key steps for navigating this stage. Then we will explore the essential discipline focused on character development and commitment. The REFINE process will help you with the realignment phase. It will help you be your best.

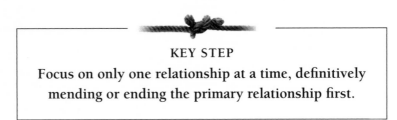

KEY STEP
Focus on only one relationship at a time, definitively mending or ending the primary relationship first.

FIRST THINGS FIRST

First things first. Generally life would be far less disrupted if you reconciled with your spouse. Your family would remain intact. Your assets would not be divided. You would not be forced to face the challenge of moving residences and on and on. But consider the other path—pursuing a relationship with the third party. Ultimately you will not be free to pursue that relationship until you finish with the obvious legal, logistical and relational entanglements of your marriage and family. Either way, focusing on the primary relationship, seeing it through till it mends or ends, makes good sense.

It also makes sense at the level of conscience. In the future you will want to be able to look back at the sequence of events and feel that you really tried to save your marriage and family. You want to feel that your efforts were not confused or halfhearted, but genuine. Furthermore, really trying to save your marriage proves your character and garners the respect of others.

Infidelity involves going in two inherently incompatible directions at the same time. People sometimes say to me, "My head says stay married, but my heart says go with the third party." If your head and heart lack alignment, you literally and figuratively experience an impaired capacity to perform or function. Consider telling the third party that you are going home to first attempt to definitively mend your marriage. Then if that does not materialize you plan to definitively end your marriage. If you end your marriage you will then be fully available for them without entanglements. Your availability without entanglements and the sheer logic of the sequence should carry weight and be recognized as valuable.

Early on in counseling, Harville Hendrix invites couples to close off all the exits to their marriage for a minimum of three month. Exits take a myriad of forms. He cites the four most extreme as separation, murder, suicide and insanity.[2] Infidelity ranks close to these in degree of intensity. Infidelity is an exit that needs to be closed in order to take care of first things first. The offending spouse needs to let go of the third party (if they have not already done so) in order to close off that exit and do the work of mending or ending. This involves a dual process of simultaneously letting go of a strong bond, while taking hold of a weak bond. It helps to keep a few concepts in mind.

- In any normal relationship, romance rarely lasts longer than a few months. If you find yourself smitten by a third party, that feeling simply cannot last.

If you think your life is complex and unworkable now, just wait: second marriages are more likely to fail than first marriages.[3] Most people jump from the proverbial frying pan into the fire if they pursue the third party.

It takes time to finish letting go of the third party. It takes time to resolve the marital and personal issues that precipitated the affair in the first place. Meanwhile, affairs often have provided a means of decreasing tension between a husband and wife. Tension—which is likely already high due to the disclosure of the affair and the ensuing crisis—may increase as you begin to focus on your spouse. Don't be confused by the tension, however; oddly enough, it provides evidence of the realignment process.

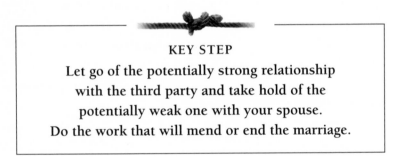

KEY STEP
Let go of the potentially strong relationship
with the third party and take hold of the
potentially weak one with your spouse.
Do the work that will mend or end the marriage.

How to Let Go

What is the best way to end your relationship with the third party? In my experience jointly written closure letters or e-mails seem to work best. Sit down with your spouse and jointly come up with a closure letter. Then send it from the offending spouse to the third party. It might go like this:

Dear Sheila,

This letter is to let you know that I'm choosing to end our relationship at this time. I deeply regret any negative impact this decision may have on you. I've decided to pursue reconciliation with my spouse, who now knows about our relationship. I fully plan on being successful with reconciliation. I will not be initiating any further contact with you and request that you not attempt to contact me. If you do attempt to contact me, I will not respond. You should receive a package containing your stuff and the gifts you gave me shortly. Do whatever you wish with my stuff. I only wish the best for you in the future.

Sincerely,
Sam

No further explanation is necessary. Often the third party is hoping that their affair will result in marriage, but alternately and perhaps surprisingly, they want an unequivocal termination of the relationship. They are thus freed to move on. All things considered, severing the relationship shows the most respect. The closure letter definitively establishes a clear boundary that should not have been breached in the first place.

As far as humanly possible, the offending spouse should not contact, talk to or look at the third party ever again. If you bonded with the third party you will experience loss and related grief. This brings us to the next topic.

UNDERSTANDING THE ROLE OF GRIEF

Just about everybody involved in infidelity experiences grief during realignment. The offended spouse may grieve the loss of marital innocence. The offending spouse may grieve the third party. The key involves learning how to comfort the grief each experiences.

Keep it simple and discreet. The offending spouse may simply say, "I'm grieving the loss of the third party." The offended spouse may find it difficult to offer comfort, but it may help to imagine what it would be like to comfort your partner over the loss of a parent. Ask,

"Is it enough that I understand or could I help in some way?" Do your best to fulfill the request or offer your closest alternative. Grief is grief, and comfort is comfort. Grief hurts; comfort helps.

CHRONIC WITHDRAWAL SYNDROME

If the offending spouse doesn't cut off contact with the third party, you run the risk of activating chronic withdrawal syndrome. Research has shown that if you stop using an addictive substance you initiate a withdrawal cycle. Each addictive substance has its own unique profile. It may take a few days or perhaps a few months for the body to normalize. You will experience withdrawal symptoms for a discrete and somewhat predictable period of time. However, if you interrupt the withdrawal cycle by again using the addictive substance, the process starts over again.

Even brief contacts with the third party can cause chronic withdrawal syndrome. Grief will eventually end unless you unwittingly relaunch the process. Stalkers, whom we have heard and read about in the news, may in part be victims of this syndrome.

Some people cannot make up their mind. One day they decide to purse the marriage and the next day (or next hour) they decide to pursue the third party. They align with their marital partner. Then they switch and align with the third party. Behavioral researchers call this phenomenon a double approach avoidance conflict. I call it the ball in the bowl syndrome. If you place a ball at the inside edge of a bowl and release it, what happens? It rolls to the opposite side of the bowl, slows near the lip of the bowl when acted on by gravity, then reverses. It rolls back and forth. Eventually the ball dies down until someone else lifts it out of the bowl. Later on in this chapter you will see how your core values, your core self, can function like a force to lift you out of the bowl of indecision before you have a breakdown. God, mysteriously and miraculously, often permeates this process with an empowering providence. God shows up and helps.

COMPARTMENTALIZATION, SYMBOL AND RITUAL

Sometimes compartmentalization can assist as the offending spouse lets go of the strong relationship with the third party. In the movie *The Prince of Tides,* Nick Nolte's character forms a strong bond with his therapist, and they have an affair. Eventually Nolte's character decides to let go of the strong relationship with the therapist and pursue the weak relationship with his wife. Nolte's character narrates a final scene as we see him driving over a bridge that he crosses daily traveling from work to home.

> I think about Lowenstein [his ex-therapist and lover] each day as I drive over the bridge. I thank her for what I learned and what we experienced. Then I leave my thoughts about her there for the tides to wash away.

Similarly, the use of symbol and ritual can assist as the offending spouse lets go of the strong relationship with the third party. In the movie *The Bridges of Madison County,* Meryl Streep's character forms a strong bond with a *National Geographic* photographer (played by Clint Eastwood), and they have an affair. Near the movie's end we see Streep's character annually going through a ritual of looking at some photos and lighting a symbolic candle as she recalls the past.

Compartmentalization, symbol and ritual used in this manner can be of benefit but also have a risk. One interpretation of the scene from *Bridges of Madison County* is that isolating thoughts about the third party to one hour a year enabled her to get on with her life, but another interpretation could be that this annual ritual kept a flame flickering that should have been extinguished years ago. Be honest with yourself. Make sure you are using compartmentalization, symbol and ritual legitimately, to control obsessions or to enforce boundaries. Ultimately, a complete break with no dwelling on the third party at all works best. Compartmentalization, symbol and ritual should serve as means to that end.

THE SAGA OF DALE AND KELLY

Dale and Kelly's story provides an example of premature and partial realignment in an attempt to ease the offended spouse's pain after a disclosure. It also demonstrates how past issues and dynamics superimpose themselves on the present situation.

Kelly struck me with her comment, "It's kind of hard to be both the enemy and the comforter of my husband." Dale, her husband, understandably had a hard time letting Kelly's affair drop. Kelly had told Dale that her affair with the owner of the bar where she worked had ended several months ago because she saw how much it hurt him and she wanted to stop his pain. But really the affair had not ended.

Dale himself had an affair five years prior, but they never dealt with it properly. Both had ongoing resentment from that and other issues. They struggled with a lack of respect, verbal abuse and underlying mistrust. Dale took control of some things like house organization because Kelly did not follow through with that responsibility. Kelly became resentful, and this when combined with a demanding work schedule at the bar caused Kelly to further withdraw and avoid issues. She'd think or say, "I'll work on that later."

As Kelly realigned to focus on Dale and their marriage, the tension between them temporarily increased. When Kelly's affair finally ended, she informed Dale, but he was now conditioned to not believe her. In an attempt to reestablish trust, Dale tried to know every detail of her daily activity. To Kelly this felt like smothering. Through the SHARE process, they made several agreements: Kelly agreed to focus on being sensitive, understanding and reassuring. She would do this by writing a closure letter to the bar owner, letting Dale review and approve of the content and message, and she would continue proactively informing Dale of her daily activities. Dale agreed to focus on being positive, to listen more to Kelly, and to let Kelly update him regarding her activities instead of pressing her for details.

Kelly let go of her strong relationship with the third party. Then together Kelly and Dale began to do the work that would definitively mend or end their marriage.

THE SAGA OF LANCE AND LINDA

Realignment requires letting go of the third party and taking hold of your spouse. Sometimes realignment requires letting go of other things that you cherish too. Perhaps you recall the saga of Linda and Lance. Linda had a yearlong affair with her neighbor, a franchise developer, sometimes rendezvousing elsewhere in Linda's car and kissing. As we worked on realignment, Linda and Lance began to wonder if they should continue to live in the home they both thoroughly enjoyed or consider moving. I asked if they wanted to treat this affair as a case of infidelity or incest.

Cases of incest present a more complex challenge than simple infidelity. Because complete and near-permanent separation proves impractical in cases of incest, the overall process is more complicated and can take longer. In the case of Linda and Lance, because they were so invested in their home and neighborhood, the third party and his wife served as a kind of extended family. Staying in the neighborhood without approaching the affair as a case of incest could prove difficult if not disastrous.

Linda and Lance felt that they wanted to primarily concentrate on one another and not further complicate an already complex process. They sold the home they loved and moved to another part of town. They sold Linda's car too. By severing their tie to their neighbors, they were able to approach the affair as straightforward infidelity, without the added complication of an incestuous "family" system. About a year later Linda and Lance had a child. Two years later they reported being at the best place yet in their personal and marital life. Realignment required letting go of something they cherished to gain something priceless.

Affairs among coworkers also resemble incest. Coworkers would be wise to find alternate places to work. Many times I've helped the owner of a company (the offending spouse) place the third party (an employee) in a comparable or better position at the company of a friend or associate. A competent employee can readily make the work adjustment. Many times I've helped people change employers, perhaps even moving to different cities. Sometimes people can stay with the same parent company but transfer internally so paths rarely or never cross.

Once I faced a situation where a combination of infidelity and some drug abuse involved five married coworkers. Their jobs happened to be so uniquely specialized that only a couple places in the United States could accommodate a transfer. I suggested we process the affair instead as an incest model. I attempted to work with all the coworkers and their spouses. Over time one of the couples dissolved and one coworker transferred. The work unit cohered again, and four marriages migrated toward wholeness.

RELAPSE

Relapse in some form likely will occur during realignment. Expect it to occur and be prepared to absorb it. Do not look at it as proof of the offending spouse's insincerity. Rather look at it as the predictable challenge associated with realignment, as the offending spouse lets go of a potentially strong relationship and takes hold of another, as the offending spouse works on comprehending and addressing the internal personal factors that powered their affair.

Perhaps most frequently the offending spouse gets seduced into a sense of obligation to be a therapist or consultant to the third party, partially out of their connection, partially out of guilt, partially out of damage control and partially out of a simple humane impulse. The bottom line remains: the offending spouse is not in a position to be a therapist or consultant to the third party.

Aaron terminated his affair with Stella. Aaron and Christy were steadily improving. Christy saw the light at the end of the tunnel and

KEY STEP
Some form of relapse is likely.
Do not try to be a therapist
or consultant for the third party.

---

started to open up again. Then one day Aaron met Stella (the third party) at the coffee shop to look at some pending legal papers for her. After their talk she came toward him to kiss him. He didn't resist her. Aaron got seduced into assisting Stella with her legal matters, and he had a relapse.

A friend of Christy's who just happened to be in the same store witnessed this scene and told Christy. About the same time Christy got some charge card account summaries. Some invoices indicated considerable spending on Stella by Aaron when they had a clandestine meeting in New York. These aftershocks wiped Christy out, temporarily demolishing several months of relationship reconstruction.

Aaron acted a little incredulous that Christy would take this so hard. He remained resolute that he wished to reconcile and rebuild. To his credit, he had met Stella in public to somewhat control the situation, but he hadn't first disclosed to Christy his decision to meet with Stella again. I explained it in simple terms to Aaron. Imagine coaxing a scared animal to make contact with you. Then imagine that just as the animal reaches out toward you, you make a loud noise and wild movement. Will the animal move closer or bolt in fear?

Realignment first takes place externally. The offending spouse stops acting out sexually with the third party. But perhaps the offending spouse and third party still occasionally exchange e-mails or have private conversations. Perhaps the offending spouse no longer contacts the third party in any form but still looks at pornography.

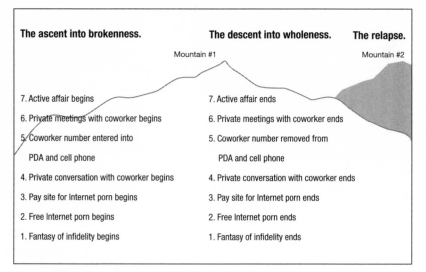

Figure 11.1 Relapse is the predictable challenge in realignment.

The realignment has taken place externally but not yet internally. In figure 11.1 six stages precede the active affair. Then the active affair ends. Externally the realignment has begun. But the internal realignment (the descent into wholeness) is only half-done. The point at which internal realignment ends is where the relapse begins. The relapse may be contained to that stage or signal an escalation. If not understood and addressed, a second ascent into brokenness looms in the distance.

THE SAGA OF TED AND BARB

When Ted was a young man he began to casually look a pornography. Later he dated and became sexually active without deep commitment to his partners. Finally he met and married Barb. Though Barb had striking beauty, Ted found himself secretly accessing Internet pornography and fantasizing about affairs. He grew closer to a female coworker; shortly thereafter they began an affair. Barb and many others felt she had a good marriage, but she found it perplexing and disappointing that Ted seemed distant and unreachable at some levels of intimacy.

Barb discovered the affair and confronted Ted, and Ted ended the affair. Barb worked hard to overcome her trauma and made progress. Some days she felt normal. Other days she struggled. Seeking reassurance on one particularly tough day, she looked at Ted's Internet history and found multiple downloads of sexual videos. She confronted Ted; at first he reacted angrily in a blend of surprise and embarrassment. Then he argued that pornography posed no threat. Later he said he was sorry for being secretive and insensitive.

Ted's downloading of pornographic videos triggered Barb. It seemed to her like infidelity all over again but in another form. Ted relapsed. When we met I drew the picture of the mountains appearing in figure 11.1. After a careful review of Ted's sexual and relational history, it became apparent that the pattern of Ted's infidelity had begun in his youth.

Some form of relapse is likely. Expect relapse to occur and be prepared to absorb it. Look at relapse as the predictable challenge associated with realignment, as the offending spouse lets go of a potentially strong relationship and takes hold of another, as the offending spouse works on comprehending and addressing the internal and personal factors that powered their affair.

One of the best paths to wholeness involves honesty. Simply talk to one another, be discrete and sensitive, but keep no secrets. Had Aaron honestly disclosed to Christy his interest in helping the third party with the legal matter, the outcome would have been different. Had Ted honestly confessed to Barb his ongoing viewing of Internet pornography, the outcome would have been different. Their internal and external realignment process would likely have progressed quicker and cleaner.

TRAITS AND VALUES

Realignment progresses best when you focus not on the characteristics of others but on your own traits and values. Michael, an insurance agent who first came to see me individually, had a severe case of ball in the bowl syndrome. One day he wanted to be with his wife. The next day he wanted to be with the third party. He talked at length about characteristics of the third party and characteristics of his wife. He talked about the pros and cons of his current life structure and the pros and cons of his future restructured life. Interspersed he made some comments about himself and his values.

As he talked I began listing on a whiteboard some of the key words he used in contrasting pairs:

dishonest	honest
unfaithful	faithful
indecisive	decisive
promise breaker	promise keeper
blended family	nuclear family
divorced/remarried	married
unsuccessful	successful
feeling-based	value-based
at odds with my faith	faith-based

After he finished speaking I wrote the words *broken* and *whole* at the top of the respective lists. Then I simply asked him, "Who do you want to be?" He said "That's me right now, isn't it—broken? Well, it's obvious: I want to be whole. I now know what I need to do." He left, and later that week he returned for his first visit with his wife.

Frankly, when Michael left I had no idea where things would go. Michael could have changed his mind. Michael's wife could have refused counseling. Either of them could have resisted change. But for the best results Michael had to base his long-term decisions on his values rather than anything else. He did, and in his case it led to marital and family restoration. A helpful list of values are compiled as the Uncommon Sense Declaration at <www.characterusa.org>.

Decisions based on values work best. Values-based decisions em-

KEY STEP
**Base long-term decisions on your values
rather than your feelings.**

power you to be your best. The next section will outline how to refine your values—to develop positive character traits and commitment.

THE ESSENTIAL DISCIPLINE FOR CHARACTER DEVELOPMENT: REFINE

The goal of refining is to be your best. We reach that goal by identifying and practicing positive character traits. Think of the traits you associate with someone. Steve has good character traits: he's honest, hard working and kind. Jason has bad character traits: he's dishonest, lazy and unkind. Character traits tend to define people and create an expectation of future behavior. We likely would stay out of relationships with Jason unless we heard him say, "I'm committed to change."

Focusing on your traits provides a road map for personal growth and change.[4] Subjectively evaluating your traits has enormous value too. After you complete a subjective assessment you can compare it to an objective assessment (such as the California Psychological Inventory) to see if they match each other or if you have some blind-spots. Figure 11.2 is a simple and easy way to subjectively evaluate yourself.

Using figure 11.2. First list your positive traits beneath the positive examples. Then list your negative traits beneath the negative examples. Finally and most important, convert your negative traits into new positive traits. To dramatize the conversion draw a line through your negative traits.

My Positive Traits (Continue to Be)

- Pleasant
- Loyal
- Hard Working
-
-
-

My Negative Traits (Cease to Be)

- Disorganized
- Overcommitted
- Quiet
-
-
-

My New Positive Commitments (Commit to Be)

- ~~Disorganized~~ Organized
- ~~Overcommitted~~ Balanced
- ~~Quiet~~ Expressive
-
-
-

Figure 11.2. Self-evaluation of traits and commitments

1. Mention positive traits often! Say to yourself "I am (positive trait). Say to others "You are (positive trait)."

2. Rarely to never mention negative traits! Avoid saying to yourself "I am (negative trait)." Avoid saying to others "You are (negative trait)."

3. Instead focus on commitments. Say to yourself "I am committed to being (new positive trait)." Say to others "I know you're committed to being (new positive trait)."

You can expand this idea by asking people you trust to evaluate you. After they have identified your positive traits and negative traits, ask them to convert your negative traits into new positive traits. Then take the next step as you progress from being to doing.

Figure 11.3 (see p. 144) is a table with three columns. Copy your composite list of new positive traits in the left column. Then in the middle column list what you could do or say to live out the new positive trait. For example:

BE	DO	WHEN
Trustworthy	Tell my partner "I'm 100-percent committed to being honest about all the details of my life." Give my partner a copy of my work schedule. Notify my partner of any changes and take whatever steps may be necessary to provide reassurances.	

Finally, in the last column identify when you will implement these changes: daily, perhaps, or weekly or twice per month. You may also identify a target date when you set a goal to accomplish a task.

Step back and look at this simple model. The positive traits which you or others already possess need to be appreciated or celebrated. So mention these traits often! The new positive traits which you would like to possess need to be encouraged. So focus on commitments! Say to yourself or others "I am committed to being (new positive trait) by saying or doing . . ."

The REFINE process has been used in this case to bring order and decisiveness to the realignment phase. The REFINE process can be used in all relationships. Recall the story of Michael, the insurance agent who could not decide whether to pursue marital reconciliation with his spouse or a relationship with the third party. As long as Michael focused on others or on the situation, he remained indecisive. As Michael focused his attention on his personal values and on his existing and new positive traits, he became empowered and decisive.

Repeat this process with your spouse and exchange results. Remember the crucial tip: never mention negative traits. Instead convert the negative traits into new positive traits and talk about them in terms of commitments. "I know you are committed to be (positive trait). Here's what you could do or say: (action and when it will happen)."

BE	DO	WHEN
"What new positive trait would be good for ME to focus upon?"	"What positive, measurable, and specific actions could I take or words could I say, that would help me be . . .	
1.	a. b. c.	
2.	a. b. c.	
3.	a. b. c.	
4.	a. b. c.	
5.	a. b. c.	
6.	a. b. c.	
7.	a. b. c.	

Figure 11.3. Implementing new commitments

RITUALS

As the realignment begins to feel stable, consider the value of performing some symbolic act or ritual. Ideally this would carry with it some drama or positive emotional intensity. Some possibilities might include a slightly more formal process of mutual confession and forgiveness:

- renewing your marriage vows
- inviting a spiritual leader to bless or sanctify your marriage and home (perhaps onsite)
- taking communion together
- burning or burying things symbolic of the negative past
- erecting or displaying things symbolic of the positive future
- taking a new family portrait
- remodeling, building or moving from your home
- taking another honeymoon or special trip
- throwing a celebration party

SUMMARY

More calamities occur on the descent than on the ascent. Infidelity involves impaired judgment; realignment provides a path for descending from brokenness into wholeness. The essential discipline for character development—REFINE—helps both partners discover how to be defined by positive character traits, which leads to value-based decisiveness. The refiner's fire separates impurities and leads to a refined state.

Rebuilding

Cultivating the Positive

Focus: Continual Improvement
Goal: Cultivate the Positive
Process: Explore the Good and Generate the Better and the Best
Key Essential Discipline: ENHANCE

After their descent, mountain climbers finally reach normal altitudes where communities can thrive. They have relationships to rebuild. Many reach a point where they say, "I'll never take those risks again. I have too much at stake. From now on we will climb as a family."

In chapter nine while discussing the revelation of the infidelity, I said typically one to three months pass from the point of disclosure to the point where a couple can begin substantive work on the marriage proper. Infidelity issues fade over time but slowly at first. Infidelity forces a demolition but also provides an opportunity to expose critical structural flaws, and to design and build a far superior structure on an existing foundation. Infidelity destroys, but I believe God can bring good out of it.

ESSENTIAL DISCIPLINES ARE REBUILDING TOOLS

The essential disciplines introduced thus far to manage infidelity prove equally useful in marriage building or rebuilding. SHARE provides the essential disciplines for communication, enabling you to understand and be understood as you take turns as presenter and empowerer. RECONCILE provides the essential discipline for conflict resolution, enabling you to explore the problem and generate solutions. REFINE provides the essential discipline for character development, enabling you to be defined by positive character traits.

- SHARE focuses on the other.

- RECONCILE focuses on self and other in conflict.

- REFINE focuses on the self.

Taken together these three essential disciplines cover an enormous amount of territory. Mastering them enables you to rebuild in a secure fashion. The following key steps will guide the rebuilding phase.

KEY STEP
Act on the belief that you can still "have it all."

Most people get married in the United States due to their attraction to their partner. A set of factors comes together to create attraction. If you ever loved your spouse and were loved by them, strong odds suggest that the components for that attraction still exist. You may need to do some serious work to open up the lines of attraction and love again, but you likely can.

To carry this a step further, if you choose to love someone, evidence suggests that you can find love. Examples of this can be found in cultures where arranged marriages still occur. My wife watched an interview of an Indian couple that married though they had not yet met. They simply said, "We did not find love; we made love." If you choose to love someone and pursue that goal with good guidance, you likely can experience love.

Finally, you dramatically increase the probability of success if you receive and implement solid professional and experienced assistance. Frankly most people receive more driver's training than marriage training. One church in our area has undertaken the development of high-quality premarital training. To be married in their church requires an engagement period, the completion of a series of classes and the development of a relationship with a mentor couple. Over five hundred couples have completed this training in the past three years. In a county where the divorce rate for the first three years of marriage is fifty of every one thousand couples, this program has a record of no divorce.[1] Competent training makes a difference.

When I meet a new couple for general marriage counseling with no reported infidelity, I ask them to guess which issues their partner would identify as significant in their relationship as I list them. People can handle criticism of themselves much easier when they report it themselves, rather than hearing criticisms from someone else. Then I ask them to add to the list from their own perspective. Usually each partner does a fairly good job identifying the other's issues. The number of issues rarely exceeds seven per person. We then begin to apply the most practical essential discipline to the issue most needing attention. Often we begin focusing on communication using the SHARE process because it provides some immediate relief. Issue by issue, whether historic or current, the REFINE, SHARE and RECONCILE processes heal—relationships progress from broken to whole. This chapter will explore the balanced and practical use of all three of these tools, and add another tool: ENHANCE.

Tough and Tender, Passionate and Practical

As you rebuild you optimize the process if you honestly stay in touch with yourself, yet remain attentive to your partner. Be strong and independent, and simultaneously sensitive and sacrificial. Each person needs to be tough and tender.

Poor communication, you may recall from chapter three, results from (1) an imbalance between self and other, (2) confused intersection management, (3) a broken, negative and problem orientation as opposed to a whole, positive and solution orientation, and (4) a lack of conscious differentiation between past experiences and present or future relationships. To be seen by your partner as strong and independent you must present your views and be understood by your partner. Conversely, to be seen by your partner as sensitive and sacrificial you must empower your partner's views and understand your partner. You both take turns as presenter, then empowerer. If your partner does not pick up on this then you model it. After a while your wholeness will become compelling.

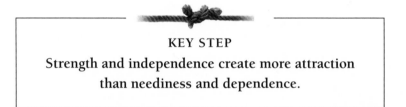

KEY STEP
Strength and independence create more attraction
than neediness and dependence.

Increase the frequency of positive experiences. Rebuilding works best when practicality and passion merge. Practicality brings order to chaos, enabling a couple to survive and stabilize. Understandably you would next long for success and significance. Passion transports you from survival to thriving.

Passion has many parts. Passion comes from alignment with your values, shared or supported purposes, and basic attraction. Attraction and desire in the end contain a few simple elements. These elements can be added to any relationship through focus and choice. Research clearly shows that similarity, proximity and reward create attraction.

Similarity comes from the conscious development of companionable features—fulfilling interests, fun activities, friends and family, faith and values, financial goals, fitness and attractiveness, and so forth. I like intense and dramatic opera, Sharon likes lighter pop music. We merged and mutually enjoy "popera" along the lines of Josh Groban and Lucia Micarelli.

KEY STEP
Attraction and desire can be cultivated by choice.
Use proximity, similarity and reward to create attraction.

Similarity can also come from making peace with how your partner simulates traits that you either liked or disliked in members of your family of origin. Acceptance or minor adjustments yield major positive results.

Proximity comes from sharing the same space and time. You live in the same home and spend time together. You go to bed at times that overlap. Sharon likes to go to bed at 10 p.m. to enjoy privacy and to read, whereas I like to write in my home office until midnight. Often enough we overlap at 11 p.m.

Reward comes from physically, mentally or spiritually pleasing your partner their way. The emotion created in the recipient—comfort, contentment, delight, enjoyment, gladness, happiness, gratification, satisfaction or joy—tests the integrity of the reward. Reward only works with no strings attached. Pope John Paul II accurately identified love as the opposite of using.[2] Reward brings people toward each other, and over time they bond.

INCREASE THE FREQUENCY OF POSITIVE EXPERIENCES

As you rebuild you must plan and think before you act. Imagine trying to build or rebuild a home without a plan, using no tools or using tools carelessly, and with inferior quality materials. You would have one bad experience after another. You would be fired and the house would collapse. The key steps and essential disciplines are your plan and tools; you, however, do the work. Positive experiences must begin to outnumber and eventually overwhelm negative experiences. Recall John Gottman's research, which identified high-functioning couples as having five positive exchanges for every one negative. Low functioning couples had closer to a one to one ratio.[3]

Lloyd owned a multistate franchise. Though he was very loving toward his wife, business demanded much of him, and Claudette—who was charming but tended toward shyness and self-consciousness—understandably grew lonely and isolated. To provide a break from the kids and an outlet for her skills and interests, Claudette worked at Lloyd's office, where she formed a playful relationship with a younger and attentive executive. There she found something she had been missing in her relationship with Lloyd. First she tried to redirect her insight to Lloyd, but he missed the cue. They grew more disconnected, and the marriage became functional only. They began to work with me.

At first Claudette denied anything but a friendly relationship with the executive. It grew deeper as we counseled. Finally Claudette acted on her emotional bond and had sex with the junior executive. It put her into such conflict with her own values and confusion about the future that she revealed it to me in a private session, then later to Lloyd. At that point Claudette only held onto a few things: she loved her children, so did Lloyd, and years ago she had loved Lloyd.

Lloyd immediately fired the executive and told Claudette that he fully planned to go on in life and find more happiness and success with or without her, though he preferred to move forward with Claudette. The choice was hers. Claudette wrote a goodbye letter to the executive, which Lloyd approved.

In therapy they focused on issues related to Claudette's affair, but along the way they developed competency with the key disciplines.

KEY STEP

**Most relationships can and will become whole and
fulfilling as both parties apply the essential disciplines.**

Claudette began to build her life around her values; Lloyd changed
the structure of his commitments so that he could be more available
to those he loved (REFINE). They took turns really pushing to understand each other and to be understood (SHARE). Why and how
did the affair begin? What role did each play in the ascent into brokenness? How did they end up in the death zone? When negatively
triggered, which still happened often, they began to explore the
problem and generate solutions (RECONCILE).

In total it took about three months for the affair and related issues
and phases to settle down. Lloyd and Claudette then used these tools
to address the marital issues preceding infidelity. They survived and
stabilized, but Claudette still lacked passion. Without passion they
would fall short of real success and significance. They began to vacation more together with the kids and alone. They bought a horse and
began training it. They introduced their children to riding, their common interest. Predictably they rebuilt love, attraction and desire.

Lloyd and Claudette started their relationship in wholeness and
innocence. Then, like many couples, they ascended into brokenness.
They gasped for air and slowly began to die. Judgment became impaired for both Lloyd and Claudette, though they acted out differently. Then on the brink of disaster they decided to descend into
wholeness. Gradually the broken gave way to whole, the negative to
the positive, the dark to the light. They reached an enhanced level
where they could cultivate the positive. Today their relationship
stands as a shelter and resource for others.

The Essential Discipline for Continual Improvement: ENHANCE

Our goal is to cultivate the positive. We do that by exploring the good and generating the better and the best.

The first three essential disciplines function like powerful work-horses to transform the negative. The next two essential disciplines, ENHANCE and ENVISION, cultivate the positive and create the possible. Most couples rarely or never assess and list the good. They rarely consciously embrace a philosophy of continual improvement. By contrast the idea of continual improvement has served many companies and corporations well. Lexus uses the motto "The relentless pursuit of perfection." A popular business book bears the title *Good to Great.*[4] Continual improvement has tremendous utility for couples too.

Use your five senses (see, hear, smell, touch, taste) to describe what your partner does or says which causes you to become positively triggered. Try to avoid reference to perceived traits, emotions, attitudes or motivation, focusing instead on what is said or done. For example:

I get positively triggered when . . .

- (I see) you make eye contact with me in a group and smile.
- (I hear) you say, "I love you and find you attractive/irresistible."
- (multi-sensory) you bring home yogurt, a movie, and freshen up with a shower.
- (I feel) you massage my back or initiate holding my hand in public.

Come up with several examples, then pick one of the positive triggers you'd like to enhance. Copy that trigger where you find number 1 on figure 12.1. Fill out the remainder of the figure; number 8 invites you to clarify the positive trait communicated in the positive trigger. This will help you or your partner to refine your efforts. Number 9 invites you to make suggestions by which this good trait

Present

1. The positive triggering comment, behavior or situation:

2. My positive spontaneous and life-giving thoughts (I think that . . .)

Positive Responses

3. I emotionally feel . . .

4. I physically feel . . .

5. I act this out by . . .

Past

6. This brings back good memories of . . .

7. This brings back good childhood memories of . . .

Future

8. I perceive the following positive traits in myself, the other person or the situation:

9. My positive, measurable and specific future suggestions that could nudge what's good into becoming better or best:

Figure 12.1. Enhance the positive

could be enhanced. In figure 12.1 we're reapplying the process covered in figure 10.1; whereas there we were working through a crisis, as we begin to rebuild we focus on the positive.

As you share the results of this process with your spouse, you cultivate the positive—you explore the good and generate the better and the best.

SUMMARY

Of the fifty largest cities in the United States, none has an elevation over 8,000 feet. Thriving communities rather are found in relatively flat areas—plains and valleys near water. Communities need resources or they will never move beyond mere survival.

Similarly as a couple descends from the harsh environment of infidelity, they can find resources for rebuilding and for thriving. In fact, with these abundant resources and successful rebuilding underway, the stage gets set for the achievement of significance—the creation of the possible.

Flourishing

Creating the Possible

Focus: Calling
Goal: Create the Possible
Process: Explore Tomorrow's Dreams, Generate Today's Plan
Key Essential Discipline: ENVISION

Jerry and Connie got married after college and eventually had two children. In their fifteen-year marriage they survived three affairs, mostly due to their love for their children and the interdependence of their businesses. Jerry ran a small but successful commercial painting business. Connie split her focus between raising the children and commercial real-estate development. Jerry handled all the painting for Connie's projects.

Jerry had his first affair with a former girlfriend early in their marriage. Connie, pregnant at the time, reacted by having an affair of the heart with another commercial realtor with whom she shared office space. Twelve years later Jerry initiated a brief affair with his secretary. With both children still in high school and their businesses even more entwined, Jerry and Connie determined that they owed it to themselves to really try before dissolving their marriage.

In our first meeting it became clear that Jerry drank too much alcohol, played too much golf and sometimes treated the children harshly. This contributed to frequent arguments and a loss of intimacy. Jerry complained that Connie seemed distant and sexually disinterested in him.

They had separated due to his recent affair and the frequency of their arguments. In the meantime Jerry had terminated his secretary by helping her get a job with an acquaintance. He regarded the affair as over.

By the end of our second two-hour session, Jerry and Connie had learned to communicate using the SHARE process. Jerry agreed to try having only one or two beers during social events for a maximum of twice weekly. If he failed at this he further agreed to stop alcohol use altogether. Connie agreed to stay together as a family at a resort over the Christmas holiday. Connie also agreed to travel and stay alone with Jerry during a mutual friend's wedding.

Though not without some flaws and stress, Jerry and Connie demonstrated measurable improvement over the holidays. This led them to ask at the next session if they should consider living together again. I asked them a simple question: "If a miracle happened and you could create the future you desire, what would it look like?" Both answered that they would have a happy and fulfilling marriage and family with each other and the kids. With some caution and reservation they each said that since their vision involved living together, and since they demonstrated the ability to communicate more effectively, it made sense to live together.

As a logical progression and a practical precaution, they learned and practiced the reconciliation process for conflict resolution. The next few sessions provided opportunity for Jerry and Connie to further master their new abilities to communicate and resolve conflicts. By the end of their ninth session of about two hours each, many old and new issues had been talked through. Adjustments and changes had been made. The marriage survived and stabilized, and their successes together mounted. Now perhaps for the first time in their marriage, Jerry and Connie were poised to pursue significance.

"With God all things are possible" (Matthew 19:26). The future calls. Envisioning enables the creation of the possible. The process involves exploring tomorrow's dreams and generating today's plans.

Cultivating the Positive and Creating the Possible

What is significance anyway? The multiple players involved add complexity to the picture.

- What do I regard as a life of significance?
- What do you regard as a life of significance?
- What do we regard as a life of significance?
- What do others (family members, friends, the community) regard as a life of significance?
- What does God regard as a life of significance?

All these questions need to be pondered and answered. The answers have some common threads:

- fulfilling relationships—working through issues of attachment and separation
- being good at something—developing an identity and competency
- making the world a better place—deciding to be whole and good (versus broken and bad), and then doing so
- making peace with God—facing the finite and the infinite

For a few years I've followed with interest the work of a researcher who set out to define the basic desires that motivate our actions and define our personalities. He has identified sixteen basic desires:

- power—the desire to influence others
- independence—the desire for self-reliance
- curiosity—the desire for knowledge
- acceptance—the desire for inclusion
- order—the desire for organization

- saving—the desire to collect things
- honor—the desire to be loyal to one's parents and heritage
- idealism—the desire for social justice
- social contact—the desire for companionship
- family—the desire to raise one's own children
- status—the desire for social standing
- vengeance (or competition)—the desire to get even
- romance—the desire for sex and beauty
- eating—the desire to consume food
- physical activity—the desire for exercise
- tranquility—the desire for emotional calm[1]

Each one of us experiences significance in a unique way—as common as a finger yet as unique as a fingerprint.[2] Among your sixteen desires, the five to seven most extreme form your core desires. They will understandably be more intense, influential and stable over time than your lesser or moderate desires. Certainly different situations can temporarily intensify a given desire at least for a short time. A starving person and an executive chef may both be preoccupied with food and eating, but for vastly different reasons. Preoccupation with food for the starving person relates to survival or security. Preoccupation with food for the chef likely relates to significance. Your core desires influence you the most, impacting your motivation and defining your personality.

In a valuable and precise way, the measurement of these basic desires fleshes out the common threads in the quest for significance. A complex interaction between inherited genetics, life experiences, the mystery of God and your choices wire you in a unique way. When a husband and wife take this inventory it becomes crystal clear that his needs and her needs will differ.

BONDING AND SEPARATION

When a husband and wife share common core desires, that bond contributes to the sense of significance. When a husband and wife differ on their core desires, they tend to separate, which contributes to conflict and the sense of insignificance.

- Principle of Bonding: Couples bond when their desire profiles are similar.

- Principle of Separation: Couples grow apart when their desire profiles are dissimilar.[3]

Attraction results from proximity, similarity and reward. Core desires form an important, if not the primary, basis of similarity.

My oldest daughter has strong basic desires for physical activity, social contact and idealism. These desires led her on an interesting early career path. For several years she worked with Outward Bound as a wilderness educator. She would take groups of twenty youth out on ten- to thirty-day courses in the wilderness. The courses provided many opportunities for social contact and physical activity. The courses also integrated idealism about the environment and the role of nature in our lives. My daughter thoroughly enjoyed her career with Outward Bound.

Along the way she met a fellow wilderness educator who shared many of her desires and values. Over time, strongly influenced by the similarity of their desires, they bonded and married. The alignment of their core desires, as well as their career paths and recreational interests, enabled them to bond and to experience significance.

In contrast, if you find yourself highly dissimilar from your spouse on one or multiple core desires, you will tend to be in conflict over that dissimilarity. If a third party comes into your life whose core desires align with your core desires, you encounter the risk of bonding with them. Kent always had a love of athletics. He played quarterback in high school. He stayed physically active throughout his life. Physical

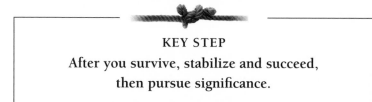

KEY STEP
After you survive, stabilize and succeed,
then pursue significance.

activity could be viewed as one of his core desires. By contrast his wife, Susan, had only an average interest in physical activity. Kent and Susan played golf together occasionally. But in their fifties Kent became even more intent on maintaining physical activity as a symbol of his vitality, while Susan had early stage arthritis and became less physically active.

Kent began to play golf in a foursome that included a competent and competitive female golfer. Kent and the female golfer shared a common passion for golf. They shared the core desire of physical activity. An affair began between them.

After the affair became disclosed, Kent and Susan found new ways to develop similarity in the area of physical activity. When they played golf Kent would hit the long balls for Susan and then she would putt the green. They also began sailing together again, which proved less physically demanding for Susan. They mutually enjoyed the sailing environment. In time Kent and Susan bonded again. They reconciled and developed collaborative solutions for their dissimilar desires.

The essential disciplines resolve many, perhaps most, negative struggles. As new issues arise couples become more adept at being their best, understanding and being understood, and transforming the negative. More resources—time, money, emotional reserves, physical energy and mental capacity—become available. This helps a couple to bond again and releases resources for the pursuit of significance.

THE ESSENTIAL DISCIPLINE TO CONFIRM YOUR CALLING: ENVISION

Imagine that a miracle occurred and life changed in a way that harmoniously worked for you and your spouse. What would that world be like and look like for you personally? This open-ended envisioning actually lets you paint a picture that reflects your core desires. As a couple confides their core desires to one another, they bond and provide a basis for insight, acceptance and strategically effective empowerment. Even differing visions or core desires, managed using the essential disciplines, can be a source of enormous enrichment.

We have unique gifts which prepare us to uniquely minister to others.[4] Each of us has a unique calling and opportunity to create the possible. Survivors of calamity repeatedly talk of thinking about something, often a loved one, to help them survive from day to day. Couples desperately need a future vision to inspire them through the work that whole relationships require. As one of my early mentors put it: "Defining the vision turns their (the couple's) energy away from past and present disappointments toward a more hopeful future."[5]

Couples begin their relationship with a dream. Along the way the dream often dies. The dreams need a resurrection. Yet practically, as you will see, while one foot rests in the future the other foot rests solidly in the present.

To comprehensively complete the envisioning process you need to identify a singular mission to unite your various roles, like the trunk of a tree unites the various branches. You also need to identify dreams or goals for each major role in your life:

- personal—your internal relationship mentally, physically and spiritually
- spousal—the relationship you have with your husband or wife
- parental—the relationship you have with your children
- familial/communal—the relationship you have with those outside your nuclear family
- financial—the relationship you have with these areas of your life

- occupational/professional—the relationship you have with the world of work

Imagining a resurrected relationship can empower you to clarify your goals and adjust your priorities.[6] Imagine that a miracle happened and you were suddenly experiencing the relationship you want. What would your miracle relationship look like? Each of you create a possibilities list for your relationship—for example: "I imagine or dream that we . . .

- regularly apply the essential disciplines in our relationship

- are accessible to each other and protect each other

- regularly and genuinely express appreciation to one another

- encourage and support each other's work and personal projects

- play together a little each day and more on the weekends

- touch often and enjoy a mutually fulfilling sexual relationship

Once you've completed your lists, take turns reading each item out loud. If your partner's first item is similar to one of yours (essentially the same even if worded differently), label both entries with the letter A. If the item doesn't match any of yours, add it to your list and label it with an A. The next similar or added item should be labeled with the letter B, and so on.

When you've both read all the items on your lists, blend what you have into one common statement. Come to agreement on the wording of item A; if you can't reach agreement, consider dropping it from the combined list. Treat the disagreement as an opportunity to practice the RECONCILE process of conflict resolution.

Once you've completed your blended possibilities list, you will have a list of ultimate dreams and goals for your relationship. Consider posting it where you will see it regularly. Read it aloud to each other once weekly.

Gradually, using figure 11.3 (p. 144) as a model, build a list of commitments to make your possibilities list a reality. For example, a list of commitments for the possibilities listed above might look like table 13.1.

Traits (BE)	Tasks (DO)	When
Disciplined	Each week focus on one of the essential disciplines until all are mastered.	All the time.
	Transfer this process into my PDA.	By the end of this month.
Accessible and protective	Call home at least once a day.	Daily.
	Keep my private cell phone on for family calls (if appropriate).	8 a.m. to 5:30 p.m.
	Meet with female clients only with a third party present, only in office or at the job site.	As required.
Appreciative	Compliment my wife about something at least one to three times daily.	Daily.
Encouraging and supportive	Teach my wife how to reconcile her new business account.	By next month.

Table 13.1. Traits and tasks in the ENVISION process

KEY STEP
**Avoid major life-altering decisions until you've
had high-end assistance for about a year.**

Don't rush this overall process, however. It took years to ascend into brokenness; give yourselves at least a year to get back to level ground. Research reveals that couples who have stayed involved in a counseling process for nine to eleven months experience the best outcomes.

SUMMARY

Couples have the opportunity to go through the stages of survival, stabilization, success and the pursuit of significance. The consistent implementation of the essential disciplines enables couples to build a foundation of security, which enables them to pursue significance—the cultivation of the positive and the creation of the possible. A couple can make it through the early stages to ultimately pursue their dreams and experience significance: fulfilling relationships, being good at something, making the world a better place and making peace with God.

Each one of us, however, experiences significance in a unique way. A failure to understand, accept and effectively respond to these unique differences spells failure. A successful couple works to understand, accept and effectively respond to these unique differences Confiding in one another about their core desires provides a basis for insight, acceptance and empowerment, enabling persons and couples to experience significance and deep fulfillment.

I greatly enjoy the little mountaineering I do. I enjoy mountain climbing much more, however, when I do it with my family. My wife meanders around the flats and reads, while my daughter, son-in-law and I summit. Mountains are a spectacle of God's grandeur; and so are families. I once ran into mountain climber Andy Politz at a friend's birthday party. These days he is breathing easy, finding rich fulfillment with his family in the flatlands of Ohio. He told me about a friend who measures his life by his summits. Andy wanted to challenge his friend: "Shouldn't your life rather be measured by the achievements of your family?" It's easy to lose perspective, but Andy knows that the path to significance comes not in the ascent but in the descent, where wholeness is found.

Epilogue

The Scientific and the Spiritual

This is—and is not—a spiritual book.

On the one hand, this book addresses the science of relationships and infidelity in particular. On the other hand, here and there I've hinted at a few spiritual perspectives. Now I want to examine in more depth the subject of infidelity from a spiritual as well as scientific worldview.

THE SPIRITUAL NEEDS THE SCIENTIFIC

A belief in God does not guarantee immunity to infidelity. Many, actually most, of my clients who struggle with infidelity also believe in God. Notable religious icons in our lifetime have succumbed to infidelity. What goes wrong?

Among several possible explanations two particularly come to mind:

- They may believe in God but may not be living for God.
- They believe in God but do not understand the impact of social science.

A simple question will illustrate the obvious. Can a person of deep personal religious faith contract a common cold? Yes. Why? Often they fail to understand or observe fundamental principles of contact contagion. If you shake hands with someone who has a cold and touch your nose or eyes before washing your hands, you dramatically increase your probability of contracting a cold.

We need to know and follow the laws of medical science or we will become infected with colds. Similarly, we need to know and follow the laws of social science, or we will become perpetuators or carriers of and victims of infidelity. It is that simple.

Sometimes people die due to complications associated with a common cold. Sometimes, both figuratively and literally, people and marriages die due to common infidelity. It is that complex.

Regardless of your spiritual fervor, the laws of science require an understanding and application of their respective fundamental principles. We need to embrace the science of relationships—the causes, phases, key steps and essential disciplines for avoiding or overcoming infidelity.

THE SCIENTIFIC NEEDS THE SPIRITUAL

Science now identifies the brains of humans as in a continual state of "seeking and wanting." One theory maintains that dreams form due to the brain's process of preoccupying or distracting our seeking and wanting system long enough for us to sleep. Pioneering neuroscientist Jaak Panksepp refers to our seeking and wanting system as "the goad going nowhere." By contrast, in the 1600s French mathematician, philosopher and physicist Blaise Pascal wrote, "There is a God-shaped vacuum in the heart of every man which cannot be filled by any created thing, but only by God, the Creator, made known through Jesus." What science sees as the goad going nowhere may be the goad to God.

I believe we have been created for fellowship with God. If we do not access that fellowship due to our ignorance, preoccupation, rejection or rebellion, we will likely experience a void—the goad going nowhere. We attempt to fill that void with literally everything imaginable. I once heard Scott Peck in a lecture refer to this process as the Eden Express. We yearn to return to Eden where we, innocent and in intimate fellowship with God, experienced fulfillment. Fellowship was broken.

Many attempt to fill the void through infidelity. Infidelity is about the broken fellowship between an individual and their partner. Infidelity is about the broken fellowship between an individual and themselves. Infidelity is about the broken fellowship between God and us.

An understanding of social science does not guarantee immunity to infidelity. My first mentor in the field of psychology eventually had to forfeit his psychology license due to having "erotic contact" with some of his clients. He knew a lot about social science, but he seemingly failed to apply what he knew. After he lost his psychology license he sought God; he overcame the infidelity and eventually became a minister. God changed him.

The spiritual dimension of the counseling experience offers a suite of beneficial factors and traditions.

Values. Those who believe in God strive for a set of values and a code of conduct. The Ten Commandments include the following:

- You shall not commit adultery. (Exodus 20:14)
- You shall not covet your neighbor's wife. (Exodus 20:17)

A preexisting deep conviction about the immorality of infidelity helps those involved end infidelity and recover more rapidly. They know right from wrong and long to do the right. A long list of similar or related values also helps: honesty, self-control, kindness, patience, long-suffering, endurance and so on.

Marriage as a holy covenant. Those who see marriage as a lifelong commitment may not even consider divorce. Lorna's husband, Ralph, recently ended a three-month affair. After we examined the causes of the affair, our attention turned to the future. Lorna began with the simple statement, "We are married." The finality of that statement led immediately to the question asked by Ralph, "How can we make our marriage good? How can we find love again?" Lorna and Ralph's sense of marriage as a covenant enabled them to rapidly shift from the crisis to exploring how to change.

Confession and forgiveness. Those who have a spiritual grounding understand the necessity of confession and forgiveness. The Lord's Prayer contains the familiar petition "Forgive us our sins, for we also forgive everyone who sins against us" (Luke 11:4). Confession and forgiveness benefit both the offending and the offended.

Two years after being shot during an assassination attempt, Pope John Paul II visited his assailant in prison to offer forgiveness. John Paul is remembered (among other things) for enduring the assassination attempt but loved and revered for offering forgiveness.

Community. A faith-based community can provide direct and indirect teaching relevant to overcoming infidelity and models of other couples who have victoriously triumphed over infidelity. Such communities offer nourishment for famished souls, simple support and encouragement, and mentors who know and care about you and can offer specific guidance.

Frankly I feel a positive and wise community may be among the most important factors in recovering from infidelity. To that end I've invested heavily in empowering faith-based communities to serve with greater wisdom regarding our culture of infidelity. I fear for couples that have no community, or worse yet a polluted community.

Supernatural, transformational power. Faith moves mountains. According to Mark 11:23 Jesus said, "I tell you the truth, if anyone says to this mountain, 'Go, throw yourself into the sea,' and does not doubt in his heart but believes that what he says will happen, it will be done for him." Infidelity builds various mountains, which must be moved. Mistrust, wounds, negative emotions, haunting images and the loss of esteem for yourself or your partner provide a few examples. Countless biblical and contemporary illustrations bear witness to impossibilities miraculously becoming reality through faith. Faith

Essential Discipline	Spiritual Principle	Biblical Reference	Social Science
SHARE	Love others	Jesus replied: " 'Love the Lord your God with all your heart and with all your soul and with all your mind.' This is the first and greatest commandment. And the second is like it: 'Love your neighbor as yourself.'" (Matthew 22:37-39)	Communication
	Listen to others	Everyone should be quick to listen, slow to speak and slow to become angry. (James 1:19) If anyone considers himself religious and yet does not keep a tight rein on his tongue, he deceives himself and his religion is worthless. (James 1:26)	
RECONCILE	Interpersonal reconciliation	Therefore, if you are offering your gift at the altar and there remember that your brother has something against you, leave your gift there in front of the altar. First go and be reconciled to your brother; then come and offer your gift. (Matthew 5:23-24)	Conflict Resolution
	Transformed thinking	Do not conform any longer to the pattern of this world, but be transformed by the renewing of your mind. Then you will be able to test and approve what God's will is—his good, pleasing and perfect will. (Romans 12:2)	
REFINE	Self-examination	How can you say to your brother, "Let me take the speck out of your eye," when all the time there is a plank in your own eye? You hypocrite, first take the plank out of your own eye, and then you will see clearly to remove the speck from your brother's eye. (Matthew 7:4-5)	Character Development (including Commitment)

The science and spirituality behind the Essential Disciplines.

Essential Discipline	Spiritual Principle	Biblical Reference	Social Science
REFINE	Individual fruitfulness	But the fruit of the Spirit is love, joy, peace, patience, kindness, goodness, faithfulness, gentleness and self-control. Against such things there is no law. (Galatians 5:22-23)	Character Development (including Commitment)
ENHANCE	Encouragement	And let us consider how we may spur one another on toward love and good deeds. Let us not give up meeting together, as some are in the habit of doing, but let us encourage one another—and all the more as you see the Day approaching. (Hebrews 10:24-25)	Continual Improvement
	Perfection	For I am confident of this very thing, that He who began a good work in you will perfect it until the day of Christ Jesus. (Philippians 1:6 NASB)	
ENVISION	Faith and inspired vision	Your young men will see visions, your old men will dream dreams. (Acts 2:17) If you have faith as small as a mustard seed, you can say to this mountain, "Move from here to there" and it will move. Nothing will be impossible for you. (Matthew 17:20)	Calling, Mission, Vision
	Faith and deeds	As the body without the spirit is dead, so faith without deeds is dead. (James 2:26)	

supernaturally and mysteriously moves mountains.

My clients certainly learn an enormous amount about the science and technology of relationships. Yet at times God penetrates all that knowledge and speaks to their souls in ways I never could. As a psychologist I know a lot about the social sciences. Yet my deepest sense of serenity, wholeness and inspirational guidance comes not from the social sciences but rather from the mystery of encountering God. God may convict, comfort or inspire me in ways that surpass all others.

THE SPIRITUAL AND THE SCIENTIFIC: A FUSION OF STRENGTHS

Mountain climbers have found one particular rope design superior to all others. The structure involves an inner or core rope that provides strength and a series of woven otter strands which amplify strength and offer protection. You cannot actually see the vital inner rope. You can only see the otter strands.

When spiritual wisdom and the wisdom of social science combine, a fusion of strengths occurs. They become woven together like strands of a rope. At the core lies an indescribable, invisible and vital force. We cannot see God but we can see the strands surrounding the core—all the eye can see, physical science, medical science, social science and so on.

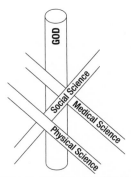

God at the core.

When climbing the mountains of life, if you wish to avoid the nearly inevitable fall of infidelity, you must use good ropes. Spiritual wisdom and the wisdom of social science form a fusion of strengths. The two are better than one.

The essential disciplines are social science strands surrounding core spiritual principles. A mountain of biblical text and spiritual tradition and a mountain of social science research support their effectiveness.

The essential disciplines, based in core spiritual principles and social science research, provide a blueprint and tools to work through and overcome infidelity but also easily transfer to all relationships and all of life. But a missing piece remains. All the social science knowledge and spiritual knowledge in the world will not exempt you from infidelity unless you submit your will to that knowledge.

James, the brother of Jesus, said something rather shocking, "You believe that there is one God. Good! Even the demons believe that— and shudder" (James 2:19). Knowledge is good, but knowledge is not the goods. Only with a personal commitment to implement these principles and practices will you experience change. For those willing to submit their will, however, James follows up with an exciting promise: "Humble yourselves before the Lord, and he will lift you up" (James 4:10). May you be lifted up.

Appendix 1
Other Paths

What if either party remains indecisive? What if the affair continues? Should you decide to end your marriage?

In my professional practice 87 percent of the couples I see regarding issues of infidelity stay married. At follow-up they consistently report being pleased with their decision and fulfilled in their relationship. What about the 13 percent who choose the other path?

If the affair continues after a brief to moderate term of joint counseling (beyond the isolated case of a predictable relapse), you should consider meeting individually as well as jointly. Meeting individually enables you and your partner to be more freely direct with your counselor or mentor about your inner struggles and experiences. At this point the offended spouse most likely needs to focus on

- letting go
- identifying their personal role in the marital dysfunction
- defining their own guiding personal traits or values

The offending spouse most likely needs to focus on

- identifying their personal role in the marital dysfunction
- identifying probable system repetition or system reversal
- defining their own guiding personal traits or values

Changing partners tends to only re-create the same kind of system.

I'm convinced that in most cases failure to repair the primary relationship creates a high likelihood of a system repetition or system reversal.

Hank found Darla to be controlling, critical and disinterested in him. So Hank started an affair with Stephanie and in time divorced Darla. Hank continued to date Stephanie, and they eventually started living together. After two years Stephanie started pushing to get married or at least to have a child. Hank dragged his feet and felt criticized by Stephanie for his resistance. At times Stephanie had a hard time being engaged sexually because of Hank's fear of another commitment. Again, though the details changed some, Hank found Stephanie like Darla to be controlling, critical and disinterested in him. Can you see the system repetition in this?

Elliot, a Jewish attorney, left his first wife because she seemed too traditional and unexciting. He ended his first marriage to have an affair with a wild and fun-seeking teacher named Cindy. Cindy did private education for elite business owners and their families. Elliot and Cindy married. Cindy liked to party and travel. Life was exciting. Then Cindy had an affair with her student's father and took off to live in South America. Elliot was not exciting enough for Cindy. The system reversed, and Cindy divorced Elliot. Now burned and cautious, Elliot found himself engaged to someone who reminded him of his first wife.

A system repetition or system reversal only delays the inevitable need to grow and change. Both Hank and Elliot desperately needed to look deeper and to address their part of the system, their part of the problem. It saves time, assets and grief to do this work in the first place.

MATCH THE TECHNICAL STRUCTURE TO THE EMERGING FUNCTIONAL REALITY

Jack, a writer of French descent and now a U.S. citizen, grew up self-conscious and confused to some degree about his identity. While very articulate and opinionated in conversation, generally with his wife, Leslie, he'd vacillate between awkward attempts to get his point across to more passive placation to not make waves. His wife pursued the arts, freely spent their money and sought out personal pleasures. Now married for ten years with two children, going in two very different directions, disaster loomed.

Leslie started an affair with a fellow art student and shortly thereafter informed Jack. Jack felt devastated, fought suicidal thoughts for a while, then secretly retaliated by forming an Internet relationship with a married female plastic surgeon out of state. Eventually Jack met with the surgeon, and their affair began. Months passed. The children and some assets formed the only common point between Jack and Leslie.

Though we met a few times jointly and several times individually, neither party demonstrated willingness to alter their path. Neither party consistently applied the relationship skills to which I exposed them. In this case neither Jack nor Leslie was trying to reconcile. The time had come to consider changing the technical structure to match the functional reality.

After a while with an ongoing affair, the marriage ceases to look like a marriage. The parties lead separate lives or may actually live in separate residences. The children become accustomed to the pattern of separation or visitation. The husband and wife only rarely consult one another. One or both parties have stopped trying. Sometimes this pattern occurs even if the affair has ended. The affair is over, but one or both parties functionally act divorced. The time has come to consider changing the technical structure to match the emerging functional reality.

How much time should pass? That question demands soul searching and careful deliberation. Some people believe that once they enter into the covenant of marriage, it never ends. They regard themselves as married and act accordingly even if their spouse continues an affair, even after their spouse divorces them, in some cases even after their spouse marries another.

I've heard some remarkable stories of reconciliation against all odds. Mike McManus, the founder of Marriage Savers, favors state legislation requiring a waiting period of one year when both parties agree to a dissolution and a waiting period of two years when the divorce is contested.[1] In states where this standard exists, such as Maryland, the divorce rate drops considerably. Seemingly during this one- to two-year period things change. An opportunity for reconciliation may present itself. Many people simply do not decide what to do until the situation forces them to decide. Moving into an official dissolution or divorce may bring reality to bear. This alone seems to motivate some people to end their affair and to try again. Generally, however, if one party refuses to try, research shows that few people can sustain a unilateral effort.

Ending a marriage has negative consequences which cannot be avoided. The various books by Judith Wallerstein should be referenced to explore more fully those negative consequences. Five suggestions, however, seem to decrease the negative consequences. In some case these suggestions actually contribute to an eventual reconciliation.

- Healing Separations
- Exploring Miracles
- Mediation
- The Good-Bye Exercise
- Individual and Family Support and Counseling

THE ROLE OF HEALING SEPARATIONS

Separations can be used to provide space for healing to occur. The partners also have opportunity to experience or preview life as a single. Some people discover that living this way does not live up to their expectations. A separation can provide a fresh perspective on many things. Optimally the couple will view this as an opportunity to explore healing and the possibility of coming back together.

It works best to literally spell out on paper the nature of the separation:

- Define the purpose of the separation.
- Disclose living arrangements.
- Agree on the handling of finances.
- Agree on patterns of child visitation or what to do with holidays.
- Agree on how to handle unexpected repairs, emergencies and so on.
- Identify when and how often you will meet and talk to each other.
- Determine if you will be sexually active or inactive with one another.
- Be honest about whether or not you will interact with a third party.
- Detail what you plan to do to grow during the separation such as joint or individual counseling, books to read, seminars to attend and so on.
- Identify people whom you expect to provide support.
- Agree to take no legal action during this period.
- Identify how the healing separation can be extended or ended.

This should be a time for the married couple to definitively mend or end their relationship; involvement with a third party further complicates the picture. The healing separation has usefulness when the couple has already functionally separated and when no progress can be made through counseling. A healing separation is an early-stage technical restructuring to match functional reality.

THE ROLE OF MIRACLES

Many times in my work with couples we could find little evidence for hope, and then a miracle occurred. Miracles both small and large contribute to the healing fabric. It's OK, perhaps wise, to spend some time waiting and praying for a miracle.

Spenser, a urologist, decided to leave his wife, Kendra, and five-year-old daughter for an ongoing affair with his nurse. He packed up some necessary personal belongings and began to pull out of the driveway to leave. His daughter, crying, ran after her daddy. At that instant Spenser recalled for the first time a repressed or forgotten memory of having lived through the same scene with his own father as a child. Spenser's parents divorced when he was quite young. Then gradually his father faded and faded until they had no more relationship. Spenser could not and would not do that to his own daughter. Miraculously, suddenly, Spenser radically changed his perspective.

Jean sat alone amidst the crowd in church listening to the speaker. The speaker said something simple yet profound for Jean. It was as if God whispered and shouted in her head at the same time. Jean knew she had to end the affair and go home immediately. Miraculously, suddenly, Jean changed all her plans.

Craig moved out and left his home and family for six months. He lived out of state with his girlfriend. Then she got fired by her employer, and because Craig had not yet divorced his wife, she decided to leave town. The person Craig could not break away from had just dumped him. In time he came to recognize his addiction to his girlfriend and the literal treasure in his wife. First suddenly, then gradually, a miracle happened.

I could go on but you get the picture. I've learned to wait for miracles. That may be your calling too.

THE ROLE OF MEDIATION

Mediation involves using a specialist to facilitate and negotiate the terms of your possible dissolution.[2] A mediator has been specially trained to help couples reach agreement.

- You spend less money on legal fees.
- You quickly face the realities of the future.
- Mediation creates an environment conducive to consideration of reconciliation.
- Even dissolving partners can more quickly become friends again.

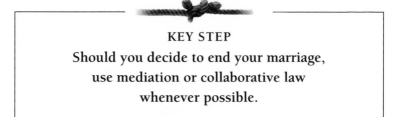

KEY STEP
Should you decide to end your marriage,
use mediation or collaborative law
whenever possible.

Clay and Erin started to divorce in the standard manner due to Erin's ongoing affair with a business associate. Clay reactively dated an attractive employee which ultimately led to a child out of wedlock. With considerable assets at stake and a very confused relationship landscape, they became increasingly bitter and argumentative. The legal bills rapidly escalated. I encouraged them to use a mediation approach to finish the process. In about two hours they reached an agreement and instructed their respective attorneys to draft papers to match. They dissolved their marriage and the dust settled. They could be polite and respect one another again. Two months later they began to date and decided to take a vacation together to explore their future potential.

Brandon and Hope dissolved their marriage through mediation at Hope's insistence. Hope blamed his controlling nature for their problems. I advised Brandon to simply say "I want to stay married to you, but since you insist on ending the marriage (and will eventually end it one way or another) I will cooperate with you." Hope started seeing that Brandon could sacrificially defer to her. They dissolved the marriage and Hope moved out of state. Brandon kept his distance, respecting Hope's need for space, but remained pleasant and available. About a year later they began to date again. In a few months they remarried and have one of the best marriages imaginable.

THE GOOD-BYE EXERCISE

During the process of ending a marriage usually one party desires to end it more than the other. Often the person most desirous of ending tends to awfulize the marriage and their partner. By contrast the person most desirous of maintaining tends to idealize the marriage and their partner. The awfulizer says "I can't stand to live with you anymore." The idealizer says "I can't stand to live without you." The good-bye exercise tends to balance out these extremes.[3]

The good-bye exercise involves the husband and wife taking turns, back and forth, responding to three open-ended statements:

I'm glad to say good-bye to . . . He says, "I'm glad to say good-bye to you always disapproving of my choices." She summarizes him, then says, "I'm glad to say good-bye to the sleepless nights wondering where you were." He summarizes her, then says, "I'm glad to say good-bye to . . ." They take turns back and forth until both have exhausted their lists of what they are glad to say good-bye to.

I'm sad to say good-bye to . . . She says, "I'm sad to say goodbye to the happy memories we have of spending summers at the beach when times were better." He summarizes her, then says, "I'm sad to say good-bye to hearing you sing to the children as you put our youngest to sleep at night." They take turns back and forth until both have exhausted their lists of what they are sad to say good-bye to in the past and present.

I'm sad to say good-bye to . . . He says, "I'm sad to say good-bye to our retirement plan of moving to the beach home permanently and growing old together and traveling." She summarizes, then says, "I'm sad to say good-bye to future easy and natural access to your family and to your dad, whom I love as my own dad." Finally they take turns back and forth until both have exhausted their lists of what they are sad to say good-bye to in the future.

This sometimes tearful exercise may take an hour or two. But it serves a valuable purpose of bringing into consciousness the bad and the good. Both usually commingle. We are all both whole and broken. This exercise helps the awfulizer to see the good and the idealizer to see the bad. Balancing the two helps.

During or after going through this exercise, some persons or couples change their path. They reconcile. Others continue on their path but with a more balanced perspective between the glad and the sad.

INDIVIDUAL AND FAMILY COUNSELING AND SUPPORT

Continue to use counseling, mentors and support systems to help throughout this painful and confusing process of ending a relationship. Choose helpers who, like you, at least support the possibility (remote though it may seem) of reconciliation. Weddings often work best when you consult a professional wedding planner. Ending a marriage similarly works out better when you consult appropriate mentors and professionals.

Once when I was a kid I went fishing with my father's Army buddy Harvey. A cast went bad, and the hook imbedded deeply into Harvey's ear. We tried to back the hook out, but the barb of the hook refused to release. Someone suggested pushing the hook on through his ear. We did this, exposing the barb, which we cut off with pliers. The hook released and we effortlessly extracted it.

If your partner gets deeply hooked by the affair, they may not be able to simply pull back. They may have to go deeper into the relationship and its reality. Sometimes only releasing your partner to go further into the affair will free them. When the time is right, your partner may come back to you.[4]

The biblical story of the prodigal (recklessly wasteful) son echoes this concept. The father in the story (Luke 15) gave his rebellious son an inheritance, which the son then wasted in riotous living until he ran out of resources. After being reduced to sharing food with swine he came to his senses. The hook released. The son returned home and in grateful humility reconciled with his father.

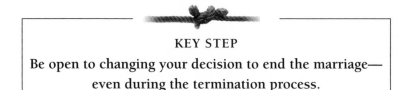

KEY STEP

Be open to changing your decision to end the marriage— even during the termination process.

Remember that early on in an affair the third party usually gets glamorized and the offended spouse usually gets awfulized. Releasing your partner to go further into reality with the third party may demystify the glamorization that accompanies the romantic phase.

Once a therapist that I greatly respected shocked me by announcing the end of his marriage to pursue a partner with whom he had an affair. Since I respected him I longed to discuss the details of his experience. He resisted talking to me for several years, but finally we met and talked. I asked him what he had learned from his experience. He replied, "After careful soul searching, I've concluded that when you end a marriage and marry someone else, in most cases— mine included—you simply exchange this problem for that problem. It's pretty much an even trade at best."

SUMMARY

When one or both parties refuse to try, eventually a functional divorce occurs. It may then be time to consider following through with a matching technical dissolution or divorce. Some people choose to end their marriage. Most likely they will end up with a system repetition or a system reversal. If you or your partner chooses this path, the hook gets pushed through. Remain open to changing your path as you gain further insight and release.

The decision to end a marriage understandably demands soul searching and careful deliberation. Be patient and thorough. Invest at least a year or two in turning things around. Do your best to insure that you contribute to the solution and not to the problem. Use the essential disciplines described in this book jointly and individually.

Regardless of whether you are the offending spouse or the offended spouse, you have choices and decisions to make. You will be tempted. You will be tried. May you be true to your values and those of God, love and wisdom. May you triumphantly overcome infidelity.

Appendix 2

Phases, Key Steps and Essential Disciplines—A Review

Phase One: Brokenness in the Family of Origin
Phase Two: Brokenness in the Peer Group
Phase Three: Brokenness in Heterosexual Relationships
Phase Four: Romantic Love
Phase Five: Civil War
Phase Six: The Evolution of Affair Conditions
Phase Seven: The Active Affair

Understanding and overcoming infidelity comes from accepting its causes, pattern and prevalence. The cause lies in our universal brokenness. Nobody is perfect; we all have flaws and needs. The pattern simply involves the loss of romance, the emergence of conflict and the risk of attraction for or bonding with another person. It is not right or acceptable, but infidelity is fairly common. You are not immune to offending or being offended.

Phase Eight: The Revelation
Goal: Understand and be understood
Process: Take turns as presenter and empowerer
Essential Discipline: SHARE

Communication usually becomes the first essential discipline couples need to master. Couples need to open up and talk deeply. The need to be understood stands among our deepest and most pervasive needs. Being understood connects to having value as a person. We want to have a sense of power. The individuals who form the couple sense and experience this as they learn to rapidly and consistently take turns empowering each other.

- In almost all cases, infidelity involves dishonesty. Honestly disclosing infidelity becomes the first and foundational step for restoring true intimacy. Honesty defines intimacy at first. Disclose the affair using the guidelines in this book.

- When too many people know about the affair the focus shifts to information management as if you were a press agent or public relations specialist. Keep the disclosure circle small—only as large as absolutely necessary for healing to occur.

- The experience of infidelity, disclosure and recovery rank among the most complex and intense of human experiences. Like surgery it is hard if not impossible to do it on yourself. Incorporate solid professional and experienced assistance throughout this process. Use assistance as often and as long as necessary.

- Often in the revelation phase the offended spouse blames their partner for the betrayal, while the offending spouse blames their partner for creating pressures and forces that contribute to their infidelity. Blame causes defensiveness and counter-accusations. Confession and seeking to understand work much better. Generally everybody bears some guilt and certainly yearns to be understood. Identify your personal responsibility and confess. Work to understand your partner. Empower each other using the SHARE process.

Phase Nine: The Crisis
Goal: Transform the negative
Process: Explore the problem and generate solutions
Essential Discipline: RECONCILE
Sooner or later people who spend a significant period of time together will encounter conflict. They need resolution of the conflict so
they can reconcile. Research has revealed a set of steps that facilitate
the transformation of the negative (the broken) into the positive (the
whole). It makes most sense to focus on the process that ultimately
generates solutions instead of polarizing arguments.

- Sticking together during this crisis has several advantages. Most
  likely you have needed more time with one another for quite a
  while. It reassures you regarding the whereabouts of one another. You literally have more opportunities to work through issues. Continue to live together with your spouse unless you are
  combatant. Tell the children something appropriate by joint
  agreement. The physical, as well as psychological, impact of
  this phase requires you to take better than normal care of yourself. Prioritize rest, nutrition, exercise and healthcare during
  this time of crisis. Get tested for sexually transmitted diseases.

- The message, the meaning, the true issues must be decoded
  amid an avalanche of emotions and ideas. The focus must shift
  from the persons involved to the causal factors and the relevant
  and related solutions. Get the message rather than (for the offending spouse) being enamored by the messenger (the third
  party) or (for the offended spouse) obsessed by the affair. Come
  to understand the developmental and marital issues underlying
  the affair. The RECONCILE process for conflict resolution systematically organizes and orders this process.

- Begin to apply the message to the marriage and be patient. Allow
  sufficient time for growth and transformation to occur. How

long? About one to three months for the crisis phase to settle, and about nine months total, enables couples to experience maximum gain and to give birth to their transformed relationship.

- The offending and the offended partner often have very different needs. The failure to fully know and creatively, adequately accommodate those needs likely contributed to the affair. Some needs may be atypical and relate only to the crisis stage; other needs may be of a chronic nature. Regardless, ask for anything, and then use the RECONCILE process to explore and generate solutions that transform. Very carefully define what it means to try; if your partner does not engage in trying to mend then consider starting to end the marriage (without beginning formal legal proceedings) as a last resort path to mending.

Phase Ten: The Realignment
Goal: Be your best
Process: Be defined by positive character traits
Essential Discipline: REFINE
While the couple learns and applies the vital skills of sharing (communication) and reconciling (conflict resolution), ultimately the turning point hinges on the values and the character of the individual. Each party faces a moment of personal truth. Who am I? Who do I want to be? Do I choose to be whole or broken? Do I choose to build my life around fundamental values or around transient attraction, emotion or the situation? Choosing to be defined by positive character traits affects the most powerful forces for realignment.

- Focus on only one relationship at a time. The logical relationship to first definitively mend or end is the marriage; it came first. Regardless of the outcome you will feel best about following this sequence.
- A romantic bond tends to have a very short lifespan. It makes

more sense, when you realize the progressively higher odds of failure in a second marriage or a third, to let go of the potentially strong relationship with the third party and take hold of the potentially weak one with your spouse. Do the work that will mend or end the marriage.

- Some form of relapse is common. Anticipating the probability of some form of relapse creates a higher state of preparedness, thus reducing damage or needless confusion when and if relapse occurs.

- For best results base long-term decisions on your values rather than your feelings. Feelings do come and go. Values come from the core of your being and ultimately, as you make decisions that align with your values, create your most enduring feelings.

Phase Eleven: Rebuilding
Goal: Cultivate the positive
Process: Explore the good and generate the better and the best
Essential Discipline: ENHANCE
The upside of infidelity is the opportunity for a recovering and overcoming couple to build a better relationship. Having worked through the revelation, the attendant crises and realignment with the previous three essential disciplines, enhancing puts full focus on cultivating the positive. Every system can be improved. Wisdom suggests the value of continually seeking to improve every aspect of your life and of others. Various fields of research converge in agreement on the overwhelming value of pursuing and extending the positive.[1]

- If you and your partner ever loved one another, you likely can again experience love. Act with the belief that if you ever loved your spouse—or if you choose to love your spouse—and if both of you receive and implement solid assistance, you likely can still "have it all."

- Most relationships can and will become whole and fulfilling as both parties apply essential disciplines—necessary practices for achieving successful relationships: character development (self-focused), communication (other-focused), conflict resolution (self- and other-focused), continual improvement (positive-focused) and the confirmation of your calling (possibilities-focused). Most relationship issues reduce down to a failure in one or more of these areas. Most relationship success can be traced back to the accidental practice or the intentional mastery of these essential disciplines.

- Strength and independence create more attraction than neediness and dependence. Self-esteem comes across to others mostly through what we say and do: "I can live with you or without you quite well, but I prefer and am committed to building a successful marriage with you. I don't expect you or myself to be perfect, but I do expect us to be making real changes that count. I believe in who we are and in what we are becoming." Act with strength and independence balanced with sensitivity and sacrifice, finding ways to empower your spouse for what they say and do.

- Attraction and desire can be cultivated. The recipe simply blends together proximity (raw time spent together), similarity (the revival of old or the creation of new common interests), and reward (whatever activates your pleasure response). When positive experiences outnumber negative experiences by about five to one, you begin to experience reward.

Phase Twelve: Flourishing
Goal: Create the possible
Process: Explore tomorrow's dreams and generate today's plan
Essential Discipline: ENVISION

We all have dreams, hopes and desires. Often life gets in the way and we lose touch with them. Or we may be clear about our dreams but despair ever reaching them. The ENVISION process both refreshes and clarifies our dreams while connecting us to today's plan and tasks. The confirmation of one's calling often becomes the last essential discipline couples master. The order could perhaps be changed in other marital situations, discussing your calling or vision first rather than last, but in the case of overcoming infidelity it's somewhat out of touch to talk about your calling or visions of significance when you're gasping for air and struggling to survive.

- After you survive, stabilize and succeed, then pursue significance. It's a progression. It's an adventure. The blessings often include fulfilling relationships, being really good at something important to you, making the world a better place and finding peace with God.

- It works best to not rush these processes. Taking the key steps and mastering the essential disciplines requires time. With each step and with all the steps, cumulatively, you progress through the stages of: awareness, exploration, commitment, implementation, internalization and finally change. So do not rush ahead to premature decisions. Avoid major final decisions until you've had high-end assistance for about a year. Work through the processes and see where it takes you.

SHOULD YOU DECIDE TO END YOUR MARRIAGE

There's a right way and a wrong way to do just about everything, even end a marriage. The termination process itself gives you a different set of data. You see in concrete terms the impact on child visitation and assets. Sometimes you see your partner, yourself or the third party in a completely different light.

Should you or your partner ultimately make the decision to end your marriage, in my experience nothing typically works better than the use of mediation or collaborative law. A facilitator ensures that both parties share and reconcile. Mediation and collaborative law often cost less, progress faster, yield better outcomes for both respective parties and engender a much more positive atmosphere than other approaches.

Several times clients have said, "We went to mediation. We talked through the details of the mediated dissolution and decided to stay together and make it work." Be open to changing your decision even during the termination process.

Notes

Chapter 1: Contours of Affairs

[1]Gallup poll, conducted May 10-14, 2001 <www.gallup.com/subscription/?m=f&c_id=10743>.

[2]D. M. Buss and Todd Shackelford, "Susceptibility to Infidelity in the First Year of Marriage," *Journal of Research in Personality* 31 (1997): 194.

[3]E. O. Laumann, J. H. Gagnon, R. T. Michael and S. Michaels, *The Social Organization of Sexuality: Sexual Practices in the United States* (Chicago: University of Chicago Press, 1994), pp. 215-16.

[4]Shirley Glass, *Not Just Friends* (New York: Free Press, 2003), pp. 3, 387.

[5]For a more comprehensive review of methodological issues, refer to A. J. Blow, "Infidelity in Committed Relationships I: A Methodological Review," *Journal of Marital and Family Therapy,* April 2005.

[6]*USA Snapshots,* February 22, 1994. Recently I met a group of men and women who want to found the Order of the Traditional Family, providing families with five-acre plots of ground, a house, a barn and gardens. They passionately believe a rural setting together with their faith and family philosophy would encourage societal restoration. Maybe so.

[7]Greenfield and Rivet, Internet Use & Abuse Survey 1999 <www.cheating-spouse-check.com/statistics.htm>.

[8]Recent research indicates that individuals who have had an extramarital affair are 3.18 times more likely to have used Internet pornography than individuals who did not have affairs. "Featured Finding," The Family and Society Database, Heritage Foundation, November 2005 <www.heritage.org/research/features/familydatabase/results.cfm?Key=635>.

[9]National Institute of Allergy and Infectious Disease, National Institute of Health, U.S. Department of Health and Human Services, November 2004 <www.niaid.nih.gov/factsheets/howhiv.htm>.

[10]National Institute of Allergy and Infectious Disease, National Institute of Health, U.S. Department of Health and Human Services, November 2003 <www.niaid.nih.gov/factsheets/stdherp.htm>.

[11]National Institute of Allergy and Infectious Disease, National Institute of Health, U.S. Department of Health and Human Services, July 2004 <www.niaid.nih.gov/factsheets/stdclam.htm>.

[12]<www.cbsnews.com/stories/2004/03/12/health/main605559.shtml>. A more conservative source, Dr. Ed Thompson (deputy director for public health services at the Centers for Disease Control), estimates that more than two million American women are infected with HPV each year.

[13]Support safe-sex education programs that emphasize abstinence and values in your schools. The program manager of the Ohio Department of Health, Office of Abstinence Education, recently requested that I develop relationship-training curriculum for teachers and teens in schools as a companion to current abstinence and sex education materials. The curriculum, Me & We, Essentially, is available at <www.stevejudah.com>.

[14]P. R. Amato and S. J. Rodgers, "A Longitudinal Study of Marital Problems and Subsequent Divorce," *Journal of Marriage and the Family* 59 (1997): 612-24; S. J. South and K. M. Lloyd, "Spousal Alternatives and Marital Dissolution," *American Sociological Review* 60 (1995): 21-35.

[15]Laura Betzig, "Causes of Conjugal Dissolution: A Cross-Cultural Study," *Current Anthropology* 30 (1989): 654-76.

[16]Glass, *Not Just Friends*.

Chapter 2: Types of Affairs

[1]David E. Scharff and Jill Savege Scharff, *Object Relations Couple Therapy* (Northvale, N.J.: Jason Aronson, 1991), p. 229.

[2]Deborah Tannen, *You Just Don't Understand* (New York: Ballantine, 1990), pp 42-43.

[3]It was not until I developed this chart that I fully comprehended the complexity involved when a person has sexual intercourse with a family member, which reaches a combined rank of 12.

Chapter 3: Causes of Affairs

[1]*Thomas-Kilmann Conflict Mode Instrument* (Mountain View, Colo.: CPP, 2001).

[2]John Gottman, *What Predicts Divorce? The Relationship Between Marital Processes and Marital Outcomes* (Hillsdale, N.J.: Lawrence Erlbaum, 1994).

[3]Steven Covey, *7 Habits of Highly Effective Families* (New York: Golden Books, 1997), p. 313.

[4]Williard Harley Jr., *His Needs, Her Needs* (Grand Rapids, Mich.: Revell, 1986).

[5]Bonnie Eaker-Weil, *Adultery the Forgivable Sin* (Seacaucus, N.J.: Carol, 1993), p. 30.

[6]Lynn F. Cherkas et al., *Twin Research* 7, no. 6 (2004): 649. To date no comparable studies have been completed on male twins.

Chapter 4: Growing Up

[1]The next four phases—romantic love, civil war, the evolution of affair conditions and the active affair—occur during the life of the marriage or committed relationship. The descent into wholeness includes its own set of phases and will be covered in part three of this book.

[2]The Reiss Relationship Profile has become my favorite assessment for identifying traits and motivational desires. It allows for the side-by-side comparison of a man and woman's patterns and hence their intrinsic compatibility. See chapter 13 for a more involved discussion of the profile.

Chapter 5: Romantic Love

[1]John M. Gottman, *The Relationship Cure* (New York: Crown, 2001), p. 19.

[2]http://web2.iadfw.net/ktrig246/out_of_cave/sss.html.

Chapter 7: The Evolution of Affair Conditions

[1]Peggy Vaughan, *Help for Therapists (and Their Clients) in Dealing with Affairs* (La Jolla, Calif.: Dialog, 2002).

[2]www.nytimes.com/2003/12/28/magazine/28GLASS.html?ex=1079413200&en=760344f129088a46&ei=5070.

[3]Shirley Glass, *Not Just Friends* (New York: Free Press, 2003), p. 33.

[4]For examples refer to the section in chapter nine titled "The Revelation Session."

Chapter 8: The Active Affair

[1]T. K. Shackelford and D. M. Buss, "Cues to Infidelity," *Personality and Social Psychology Bulletin* 23 (1997): 1034-45.

Chapter 9: The Revelation

[1]David E. Scharff and Jill Savege Scharff, *Object Relations Couple Therapy* (Northvale,

N.J.: Jason Aronson, 1991), p.218

[2]The next section will outline how to SHARE effectively in more detail. The CD and guidebook *Essential Disciplines for Communication—SHARE* can be ordered by phone at 1-800-837-SEEK or from our website at <www.EssentialDisciplines.com>.

[3]My hour-long video *Staying Together* digests the contents of this book and helps a couple rapidly grasp the bigger picture behind the affair. It can be ordered by phone at 1-800-837-SEEK or from our website: <www.EssentialDisciplines.com>.

Chapter 10: The Crisis

[1]During my graduate training I received formal training and did research with a procedure known as Rational Stage Directed Hypnotherapy (RSDH). RSDH employs elements of exposure therapy, relaxation therapy, cognitive restructuring and hypnosis. These therapies have been shown to be of value in the treatment of PTSD or related symptoms.

[2]Rational Stage Directed Hypnotherapy (RSDH).

[3]Current research reveals that those who sustain a marriage have an average two times the personal net worth of those who divorce. Those who divorce on average lose 77 percent of their assets due to asset division and increased costs <http://researchnews.osu.edu/archive/divwlth.htm>.

[4]Janis Abrahms Spring, *After the Affair* (New York: Harper Collins, 1996), p. 30.

Chapter 11: Realignment

[1]The Reiss Profile and the Reiss Relationship Profile, which get further discussion in chapter 13, literally measure your orientation toward honor/expediency on a scale so named. You may complete this 16-scale profile at <www.EssentialDisciplines.com>.

[2]Harville Hendrix, *Getting the Love You Want* (New York: H. Holt, 1988), pp. 86-97.

[3]First marriages fail at around a 50-percent level and second marriages at a 60-percent level.

[4]The California Psychological Inventory provides a good, comprehensive and objective assessment of your traits. You may directly access this assessment online through my website: <www.EssentialDisciplines.com>. Refer also to pages 52-53 regarding the California Psychological Inventory.

Chapter 12: Rebuilding

[1]Rich Nathan and Ron Hitchcock, Vineyard Columbus, 2004.

[2]Karol Wojtyla, *Love and Responsibility* (New York: Ignatius, 1993), pp. 28-31.

[3]John M. Gottman, *The Relationship Cure* (New York: Crown, 2001), p. 19.
[4]Jim Collins, *Good to Great* (New York: Harper Business, 2001).

Chapter 13: Flourishing
[1]Steven Reiss, *Who Am I? The 16 Basic Desires That Motivate Our Action and Define Our Personalities* (New York: Tarcher/Putnam, 2000), pp. 17-18.
[2]You may find it interesting and helpful to take this inventory at this time. It enables you to measure the relative strength of your 16 basic desires. The Reiss Inventory can be taken and immediately interpreted for you in the Assessments section of our website at <www.EssentialDisciplines.com>.
[3]Reiss, *Who Am I?* p. 143.
[4]If you have not already done so, reading *The Purpose Driven Life* by Rick Warren offers powerful insight into finding your vision and purpose.
[5]Harville Hendrix, *Getting the Love You Want* (New York: H. Holt, 1988), p. 89.
[6]This process is beyond the scope of this book. Our focus is the marital relationship. The CD guidebook *Essential Disciplines for Calling, Purpose and Passion—Envision* can be ordered by phone at 800-837-SEEK or online at <www.EssentialDisciplines.com>.

Appendix 1
[1]Mike McManus, conference call, November 11, 2005.
[2]Collaborative law, though using two attorneys, follows the same principles as those used in mediation.
[3]I learned of the good-bye exercise from my early mentor Harville Hendrix.
[4]This theme is repeated, perhaps more bluntly, in 1 Corinthians 5:5: "Hand this man over to Satan."

Appendix 2
[1]David L. Cooperrider, Peter F. Sorensen Jr., Therese F. Yaeger and Diana Whitney, eds., *Appreciative Inquiry: An Emerging Direction for Organization Development* (Champaign Ill.: Stipes Publishing L.L.C., 2001).